Hudson River

HENRY HUDSON PARKWAY

RIVERSIDE DRIVE

WEST END AVENUE

BROADWAY

AMSTERDAM AVENUE

Lincoln Centre

COLUMBUS AVENUE

Natural History Museum

CENTRAL PARK WEST

Central Park

Metropolitan Museum of Art

FIFTH AVENUE

MADISON AVENUE

PARK AVENUE

LEXINGTON AVENUE

THIR

SECO

FIRS

D1225207

YORK AVENUE

FRANKLIN D. ROOSEVELT DRIVE

EAST END AVE

JEENSBOROUGH

scale of main map

0   ¼   ½ mile
0   ¼   ½   ¾ kilometre

Art centers of the world — New York

General Editor: G. S. Whittet

Art centers of the world New York

Randolph E. Osman

The World Publishing Company
Cleveland and New York

Designed and produced for The World Publishing Company,
2231 West 110th Street, Cleveland, Ohio 44102
by George Rainbird Ltd, Marble Arch House,
44 Edgware Road, London W2
Phototypeset by V. Siviter Smith and Co. Ltd,
Birmingham 12, England
Printed and bound by Grafoimpex, Zagreb, Yugoslavia
House Editor: Mary Anne Norbury
Typographer: John Wallis
Endpapers: John Flower

First published 1968

Printed in Yugoslavia

Contents

Photographic credits and acknowledgements

The publishers and producers wish to express their gratitude to the museums and photographers who have courteously assisted the author in obtaining the material for illustrations reproduced in this book. Further they would like to include additional information appertaining to the works of art reproduced which the captions by reason of space are unable to contain. The Metropolitan Museum of Art: Anonymous gift 2, 1932; Rogers Fund 3, 1906; 7, 1919; 9, 1928; 11, 1952; 12, 1960; 30, 1926–31; The Jules S. Bache Collection 4, 1949; 6, 1949; II, 1949; Fletcher Fund 5, 1933; 32, 1947; Gift of J. Pierpont Morgan 8, 1916; 35, 1920; Leland Fund 10, 1913; Gift of Henry G. Marquand 13, 1889; Gift of Harry Payne Bingham 14, 1937; The H. O. Havemeyer Collection 15; 18; 19; 22; 23; Bequest Mrs H. O. Havemeyer 18, 1929; 19, 1929; 23, 1929; Gift of Horace Havemeyer 22, 1929; Catherine D. Wentworth Fund 16, 1949; Wolfe Fund 17, 1931; 20, 1907; 26, 1906; Purchased with special funds and gifts of friends of the museum I, 1961; Gift of William Church Osborn 21, 1949; Bequest Samuel A. Lewisohn 24, 1951; Gift of Thomas F. Ryan 25, 1910; Arthur H. Hearn Fund 27, 1950; George A. Hearn Fund 28, 1933; Bequest Michael Dreicer 29, 1921; Museum Excavations 30, 1926–28; Bequest of Richard De Wolfe Brixey VII, 1943; Alfred Stieglitz Collection X, 1949. The Cloisters: Purchase 39, 1963; 40, 1954; Gift John D. Rockefeller, Jr III, 1937. The Museum of Modern Art: Lillie P. Bliss Bequest VI; acquired through the Lillie P. Bliss Bequest 60; Gift of Nelson A. Rockefeller 56; Mrs Simon Guggenheim Fund 57; 68; museum purchase 62; 64; 66. Courtesy the Thannhauser Foundation, New York 73. Photo Catherine E. Struse-Springer 31. Photo Eric Pollitzer 48; 100; 115; 116; 117; 119; 121. Alexandre Georges 54. Ezra Stoller (Esto) 92; 93.

The author wishes to express sincerest thanks to the friends and museum staff members who aided him in countless ways while writing this book. A note of special gratitude goes to Sabrina Longland who edited much of the manuscript, wrote a number of passages herself and saw the book through its final stages. Thanks are also due to Diane Kunde who typed and retyped the various drafts.

R.E.O. September, 1967

List of color plates

List of illustrations

Introduction

No other city in America offers the amount and variety of superb art to be found in New York, while her universities, art schools, museums, art galleries, libraries, film centres and large group of publications combine to create an environment at once dynamic and stimulating both for the artist and for his public alike.

The museums themselves, the main concern of this book, in the nature of their collections, reflect the diversified loves and interests of the City's great collectors and benefactors as well as of the people of all backgrounds who make these museums' abiding patrons: the Museum of the American Indian, the Jewish Museum, Asia House, the Hispanic Museum, are just a few examples. Several museums, including the Metropolitan, the Brooklyn and the Modern offer full cultural programmes consisting of lectures, films, concerts, publications, guided tours, classes in studio art and training for prospective curators. Both the Metropolitan and the Brooklyn Museum have outstanding programmes designed especially for children. Indeed, the old stereotype of a museum as a dark and forboding storehouse for heirlooms, curiosities and rich men's tax deductions is as outmoded as the ankle-length hem line. With modern lighting, display techniques and educational facilities, and with the wide range of related activities, most of the City's museums are as busy as its hospitals, and many now have evening hours to accommodate increased attendance.

This book, designed for the general reader, joins happily in the present trend toward a more thorough understanding of mankind through a closer familiarity with great works of art. Some of the finest examples of the various schools are selected from museums having permanent displays. An effort is made to discuss not just painting, but the other arts too, and wherever possible to sketch in some relevant background in an attempt to achieve a semblance of historical continuity through each museum. Hopefully this will facilitate the reader in evaluating the work of art relative to the time and circumstances under which it was created. Many of the works are illustrated, but all of them must be seen at first hand, and therefore pure verbal description is kept to a minimum in the belief that no amount of words can replace the visual experience itself. A section towards the end of the book entitled 'Out of doors and incidental' is devoted to architectural and sculptural monuments not housed in museums. There is also a short section on where to buy works of art in New York, with a selected list of commercial galleries including addresses and telephone numbers.

New York abounds in art shows, gallery openings, public lectures and exhibitions, most of which find extensive listing and coverage in the 'New York Times' and 'Cue Magazine.' 'The Village Voice' covers the more *avant garde*. The City's three main art reference libraries— the Frick, the Metropolitan, and the Art and Architecture room of the Public Library at 42nd Street and Fifth Avenue — are open to interested adults.

Artist's dates, given at the first mention of the artist generally follow those found in Peter and Linda Murray's *A Dictionary of Art and Artists*. For the dates of individual paintings and other works the various museum publications listed under *Credits* have been consulted.

Metropolitan Museum of Art

Fifth Avenue at 82nd Street
IRT Subway (Lexington) 86th Street Station; Fifth Avenue
Buses 2, 3, 4

The Metropolitan Museum of Art, one of the greatest institutions of 1
its kind in the western world, is not the result of the passing on of royal
treasure troves, nor of the spoils of war. It was created by free individuals, out of private funds, and turned over to the public in one of
the great gestures of American philanthropy. As a place to study, to
rest, to become inspired, or excited, or confused, to find out what
Egyptians wore or what kind of painting corresponds to the Beatles'
music, there is no better place in the country. The museum is the
fourth largest in the world, with collections that document some 5,000
years of man's history with the objects he created. To follow the thread
of cultural evolution that leads from Queen Hatshepsut to Larry Poons
– for those who have imagination – can and should be a vigorous and
rewarding experience.

The history of the Metropolitan begins properly with an after-dinner
speech given on July 4, 1866, in Paris, by the American statesman
John Jay, in which he called on the American people to lay the
foundations for a 'National Institution and Gallery of Art.' A committee
was formed and a letter was addressed to the Union League of New
York urging the foundation of 'a permanent national gallery of art and
museum of historical relics –. ' The Union League held a meeting on
October 14, 1869, at which William Cullen Bryant acted as president
and gave the opening speech. A resolution was adopted to establish
' . . . in this city . . . a museum of art, on a scale worthy of this metro-
polis and of a great nation.' Letters were sent out to authorities on the
matter asking for advice on organization. In reply to a request asking
for his counsel with reference to what kind of man should govern the
new museum, the Rev. Dr Henry W. Bellows in a letter dated January

1. The Metropolitan Museum of Art

7, 1870, replied, 'It wants men of middle age, of unabated energy, resolute will, and hot enthusiasm to carry forward such a work . . . men of art-culture and positive art knowledge.' Thus a precedent was set for future museum directors from General Louis Palma di Cesnola, the first, through numerous men of outstanding 'art-culture', including James J. Rorimer whose untimely death in 1966 was deeply felt throughout the international art world. The latest to date is Thomas P. F. Hoving, former director of the Cloisters, former Commissioner of Parks, and the youngest man ever to hold the august position.

In April of 1870 New York State granted a charter to the museum, and in May a permanent constitution was adopted. From 1871 to 1873 the Metropolitan occupied the Dodworth Building, a converted dancing academy on Fifth Avenue between 53rd and 54th Streets. From 1873 to 1879 it was relocated in the Douglas Mansion at 128 West 14th Street.

It was not until 1880, nearly ten years after its inception, that the Metropolitan moved to its present and permanent location in Central Park. The original two-storey red brick building, conceived in part by Calvert Vaux, designer of Central Park itself, is today the West Wing. The central part of the present building, Roman eclectic in style, with its massive pairs of columns, was designed by Richard Morris Hunt, famed builder of Newport residences and of the Tribune Building in New York. It was completed by his son in 1902. The north and south wings were added in 1905–1916 by the dean of American architectural firms, McKim, Mead and White. The façade was never completed, however, and atop the four pairs of columns where there were to be sculptured groups representing the four great epochs of art — Egyptian, Greek, Renaissance, and Modern — there now stand only grey blocks of stone. In 1924 the American Wing was added, and by 1970 there will be a ground-breaking ceremony for an entirely new American Wing building.

The Metropolitan's 100th Anniversary, to be celebrated in 1970, will see a grand re-organization and expansion programme. Along with the new American Wing, there will be a gallery of musical instruments, a new gallery of Pre-Colombian Art, a Greek and Roman Gold Room, and major additions to the Oriental and Egyptian galleries. The main entrance and the Great Hall will also be re-organized.

The entire collection cannot be seen in one visit, and it is the wise visitor who choses one or two areas each time, and no more. The most noted collections are the Egyptian, Greek and Roman art, European paintings, Arms and Armor, and American paintings.

European paintings number over 2,000, of which about 900 are exhibited at any given time. The following discussion will, as far as possible, proceed chronologically and by national school. With the exception of the Bache and the Altman Collections, paintings of the same school and period are usually found together. The numbers next to a painting and preceeding its date refer to the gallery in which it is normally located. Naturally, with such a large collection, it is possible to discuss only certain aspects of selected examples; the choices have usually been made on the basis of quality, historical importance, and uniqueness within the collection, in that order.

The founder of modern painting is generally regarded to be the Florentine painter Giotto (probably 1266/1267–1337), for it was he who first imbued his human and animal figures with a new life, a sense of weight and depth, a personality and individuality foreign to the predominant Byzantine style, with its two-dimensionality, its stylized figures and gold backgrounds. Very few of Giotto's paintings exist outside Italy; the Metropolitan's small *Epiphany* (11) is from the master's shop, if not by his own hand. It is part of a series of paintings on the life of Christ. For style, it may be compared with the 13th century Florentine panel in the Byzantine style hanging next to it.

Where the Byzantine painter follows a tradition almost 500 years old in the painting of faces and draperies, Giotto is a revolutionary; he transforms the stiff, posed movements of people into natural actions; he abandons the traditional stylized drapery for a new, volumetric one; he places his figures in tiers to show distance from the foreground, creating a sense of place, of time, and of intimacy among his characters.

The radical new achievements that Giotto brought to the art of painting were not everywhere accepted at once. In Siena, and especially across the Mediterranean in Spanish Valencia, those who commissioned paintings were less willing to relinquish the older, more conservative, styles. A tall panel showing *The Trinity Adored by All Saints* (28) is by an unknown Valencian painter of the early 15th century. Although it is more than a hundred years later than Giotto's *Epiphany* it is far more medieval and 'Gothic' in feeling. There is almost no attempt to show space, figures are lined up along the picture plane; a star-spotted blue background hangs like a curtain behind the figures.

The Sienese painters of the late 14th and early 15th centuries were more romantic, gentle and aloof than their Florentine contemporaries. About 1400, when the lyric, aristocratic International Style, emanating from the court of the Dukes of Burgundy, became widespread in

Western Europe, the Sienese continued it well into the 15th century.
3 A good example is the little panel of *Paradise* (28) by Giovanni di
Paolo (1403–1482/1483), painted about the middle of the century,
reminiscent of tapestries, richly decorated and hung on the walls of
royal chambers.

The great innovations of the early Renaissance were made first by
sculptors, not painters. And so it is that we quite rightly see the
accomplishments of Donatello and Ghiberti incorporated into the
Saint Sebastian (27), *c.* 1445, by Andrea del Castagno (*c.* 1423–
1457), one of the most influential Florentines of the generation following Masaccio – the young genius who is the logical heir to Giotto.
Saint Sebastian was shot full of arrows (symbols of disease) by the
Roman Emperor Diocletian. His miraculous endurance of them caused
him to be venerated for his powers to resist disease, and this painting
may have been commissioned as an act of gratitude for his inter-
vention against the plague, a major threat to life at the time.

One of the most interesting of all the stories told by Vasari (16th
century painter-historian) is that of the Florentine Piero di Cosimo
(*c.* 1462–1521?) whose two panels, *A Hunting Scene* and *The Return
From the Hunt,* (27), *c.* 1490, were among the first paintings acquired
by the Metropolitan. Vasari relates that Piero was especially interested
in the bizarre aspects of nature, in plants and animals shaped
strangely, that later in life he became a recluse, letting his yard become
overgrown with vines and living entirely on eggs boiled fifty at a time;
that his contemporaries considered him mad. His two panels have

2. Andrea Mantegna,
*The Adoration
of the Shepherds,*
c. 1460
tempera on canvas,
transferred from wood
15¾ × 21⅞ in.
(39·3 × 55·5 cm.)

3. (left) Giovanni di Paolo, *Paradise, c.* 1450
tempera on canvas, transferred from wood $18\frac{1}{2} \times 16$ in. $(46 \cdot 9 \times 40 \cdot 6$ cm.)
4. (right) Domenico Ghirlandaio, *Francesco Sassetti and His Son Teodoro,* 1487–89
tempera on wood $29 \times 20\frac{1}{2}$ in. $(74 \cdot 9 \times 52$ cm.)

been thought by Professor Panofsky to be part of a series representing
the growth of civilisation through control of fire.

One of the most passionate devotees of archaeological studies in
the Renaissance was Andrea Mantegna (*c.* 1431–1506) of Padua,
an adopted son and pupil of the archaeologist-painter Squarcione.
The Adoration of the Shepherds (28), *c.* 1460, is from the artist's early
period, and though it fails to make the specific references to classical
antiquity that some of his later paintings do, Joseph's sandals are
Roman in type and his pose is thoroughly antique. The expressive use
of line and the incredible detail are characteristics of Northern Italian
painting. Mantegna's realism, more specific and detailed than that of
his brother-in-law, Giovanni Bellini, proceeds from his passionate
interest in the world of things, of textures, of space and colour.

One moves quite easily from this work to *The Meditation on the
Passion* (2) which still bears Mantegna's forged signature on the
lower right. By the Venetian Vittore Carpaccio (*c.* 1455–1523/1526),
it was long thought to be a Mantegna. The scene shows Job (on the
right) and St Jerome (on the left) meditating on the Passion of Christ

who is seated in the centre on a dilapidated Renaissance throne.

The early Renaissance, as part of its awakened interest in the
4 individual, was naturally concerned with portraiture. *Francesco
Sassetti and His Son Teodoro* (12), 1487–1489, by Domenico
Ghirlandaio (1449–1494) is an excellent example of Florentine
portraiture in the last quarter of the 15th century. Sassetti was a
wealthy businessman, a partner in the Lyons bank of the great
Lorenzo de'Medici, and this portrait, one of several that Ghirlandaio
did of him and his family, shows him serious and immobile, while his
little son looks at him with a kind of reverent wonder. Another
Florentine portrait is that by Lorenzo di Credi (*c.* 1458–1537) which
is supposed to be of Ginevra de'Benci (b. 1456), entitled *Portrait of
a Lady* (26). Ginevra was also painted by Leonardo in the famous
Washington National Gallery portrait.

Carlo Crivelli (d. 1495) was a Venetian by birth, but did most of his
work elsewhere. He was fond of Mantegna and of Northern late
Gothic painting and sculpture. A more emotional, flamboyantly
dramatic and intensely pietistic painting than his *Pietà* (27), *c.* 1485,
can hardly be imagined.

One need only move a few yards to the *Madonna and Child* (12),
c. 1483–1490, by the true Venetian Giovanni Bellini (1430–1516) to
see how 'Gothic' and Northern in feeling is the Crivelli. Crivelli's hard
line becomes soft *sfumato* as edges blend quietly into adjoining surfaces. The Bellini speaks a different language from the Crivelli, the
latter quick, colloquial and anecdotal, and the former, rich, classic,
and lyrical. The same might be said for the other Bellini *Madonna and
Child* (2), *c.* 1460–1462, which, though in rather a poor state of preservation, and earlier, is a beautiful and majestic work.

The other great centre of artistic activity in the 15th century was
Flanders, principally the city of Bruges; and the most famous name in
Early Flemish painting is that of Van Eyck. The Metropolitan has no
works unquestionably by Jan van Eyck (d. 1444), considered the
founder of the school, but the two small panels of the *Crucifixion* and
Last Judgment (10) are generally considered to be the work of Jan's
supposed older brother, Hubert. The paintings were purchased in
Spain by a Russian Ambassador prior to 1840, at which time there
was a central panel (now lost) showing the *Adoration of the Magi.*
The Metropolitan bought them from the Hermitage Museum in
Leningrad in 1933. Probably done sometime during the teens of the
15th century, these panels (now transferred to canvas) are prime
examples of late Northern Gothic painting. Every square centimetre

5. (left) Hubert van Eyck, *The Crucifixion* and *Last Judgment,* 1410–20
tempera and oil, transferred from wood each panel $22\frac{1}{4} \times 7\frac{3}{4}$ in. (56.5×19.6 cm.)
6. (right) Petrus Christus, *Portrait of a Carthusian Monk,* 1446
tempera and oil on wood $11\frac{1}{2} \times 8$ in. (29.2×20.3 cm.)

of the surface is covered with infinite detail. Nothing is left to the imagination; the horrors of Hell are shown in the most graphic manner — as if the painter had seen it all himself. In fact one is aware of no distinction whatsoëver, in manner of representation, between the temporal world of the Crucifixion and the atemporal worlds of Heaven and Hell — everything is treated with the same unflinching realism. The vigor of Van Eyck's imagination along with his unequalled mastery of the technique of painting combine here to produce one of the outstanding masterpieces in the museum.

Interest in portraiture was even more pronounced in Flanders than it was in Italy. Certainly the most remarkable Early Flemish portrait in the museum is that of a *Carthusian Monk* (15) signed and dated in 6 1446 by Petrus Christus (d. 1472/1473), a pupil and follower of Jan van Eyck. Realism is here carried to a logical extreme; it could and would go no farther. The painting is almost shocking in its life-like quality, achieved by the use of needle-like brushes. The uncanny penetration of character has rarely been surpassed in any painting.

While Christus followed the highly realistic and detailed style of Jan van Eyck, Roger van der Weyden (1399/1400–1464), the greatest painter of mid-15th century Flanders, laid emphasis on significant action and simplification of formal elements. His portrait of *Francesco d' Este* (10), *c.* 1460, in the simplified planes of the face, the flattened chest, the prominent nose and eyes and the thin shadows, contrasts markedly with the *Portrait of a Carthusian Monk.*

29 In *Christ Appearing to His Mother* (10), 1440–1445, Roger shows an interest in drama and emotion unlike the restrained works of the Van Eycks. The shock value of the resurrected Christ's unexpected appearance at the side of his mother, who had been quietly reading, is enhanced by a stark contrast in colour between the two robes and by the gesticulating hands. Through an open door in the background we see the Resurrection itself, while the Old Testament prefigurations for it are sculpted on the four capitals inside the chapel. The sculptured scenes on the arch depict events in the life of the Virgin.

Few painters were more highly regarded by the 19th century than was Hans Memling (d. 1494) a pupil of Roger's. His sweet and charming portraits, however, add little to what they take from his teacher and consequently have declined in popularity during the present century. Nevertheless, the *Portrait of an Old Man* (13) is remarkable for its technical competence; and the two portraits of *Tommaso and Maria Portinari* (3), *c.* 1472, are important as works by the most popular painter of the day commissioned by one of the wealthiest and most prominent patrons.

The last of the great painters of Bruges, before this city gave way to Antwerp as artistic capital of the North, was the Dutch-born Gerard David (d. 1523). The *Rest on the Flight into Egypt* (15) is an exquisite little painting, perfectly balanced, with a beautiful landscape in the background. It is often overlooked in favour of a more recent acquisition, two panels of the Annunciation; the *Archangel Gabriel* and the *Annunciate* (10), *c.* 1520.

Joachim Patinir (d. *c.* 1524) was the first Fleming to become deeply interested in landscape for its own sake, and it is upon his work that the great 17th century Flemish landscape tradition rests. *The Penitence of St Jerome* (7), *c.* 1500–1524, displays his masterly ability to achieve an unbroken recession into infinitude, unlike earlier works where a sharp division is made between foreground and background. The left panel shows the Baptism of Christ; the right shows St Anthony tempted by Bosch-like monsters. In the central panel St Jerome kneels before a crucifix. In the near distance is an illustration

7. Pieter Bruegel the Elder, *The Harvesters*, 1565
oil on wood   46½ × 63¼ in. (118·1 × 160 cm.)

of the legend of Jerome's friendly lion who, after Jerome removed the thorn from his foot, was accused of stealing and eating a donkey. The lion is seen having exonerated himself by finding the donkey, which was in fact stolen by the thieves who are shown before the abbot kneeling and begging forgiveness.

Pieter Bruegel the Elder (d. 1569) carried the Flemish landscape tradition into the 16th century with his *Harvesters* (7), 1565, one of the museum's most popular paintings. The tradition of representing the months of July and August by a harvest scene occurs in sculpture on Gothic cathedrals and in many illuminated calendars. Bruegel painted four additional scenes representing other months, of which *Hunters in the Snow* (Vienna) is the most famous. He was widely known in his own day for his satirical engravings, and an element of satire may be detected in the spread-eagle pose of the man in the foreground. The painting as a whole, however, shows a sincere interest in the mores of peasant life, a fascination with nature, and a concern with rich colour and nearly abstract form that seems to foreshadow

8. (left) Raphael, *The Colonna Madonna, c.* 1504–5
tempera on wood 66⅝ × 66¾ in. (169·1 × 169·5 cm.)
9. (right) Lucas Cranach the Elder, *The Judgment of Paris, c.* 1528
tempera and oil on wood 40⅛ × 28 in. (101·9 × 71·1 cm.)

Van Gogh in the 19th century.

 American museums are notoriously weak in paintings from the period of Italian art known as the High Renaissance (from about 1500 to *c.* 1527). In fact the Metropolitan has no works by Leonardo or Michelangelo, and only one by Raphael (1483–1520), youngest of the three founders of the style.

8 Raphael's large *Colonna Madonna* (1), *c.* 1504–1505, though completed prior to his Roman period, must serve as the museum's nearest example of the High Renaissance. The four saints – Peter, Paul, Catherine, and Cecilia – are grouped around the Madonna with the infant Jesus and John the Baptist in a perfectly symmetrical manner. The diagonal lines of the throne converge exactly on the horizon, just as lines drawn through the heads of the four saints would converge at the top of the picture plane; thus, all is order, harmony and balance, a controlled recession into space.

 Certainly the greatest of the Venetian painters was Titian (1487/ 1490–1576), whose extraordinarily long span of activity and growth as an artist caused him to be sought out by the Venetian state, the courts of Ferrara and Mantua, and by the the Emperor Charles V, and

0. Jacopo Tintoretto, *The Miracle of the Loaves and Fishes, c.* 1544–47
il on canvas 61 × 160½ in. (154·9 × 407·6 cm.)

Philip II of Spain. The *Portrait of Filippo Archinto, Archbishop of Milan* (4), *c.* 1554, shows Titian's remarkable ability to capture the depth of character of his sitters. Archinto was forced into exile by political enemies, never to return to his native Milan, and Titian seems to have painted a tormented longing into his expression. *Venus and The Lute Player* (2), *c.* 1562–1565, is a work of the artist's old age, as we know from the subdued tonality of the colours, the broad and easy handling of forms, and the deliberately unfinished areas. The golden light that surrounds the figures and bathes the landscape is a hallmark of Venetian painting. Venus herself represents beauty; the small cupid crowns her with love while musical references abound.

Mars and Venus United by Love (1) by Paolo Veronese, (*c.* 1528–1588), illustrates the enormous preoccupation with classical myth and allegorical detail rendered in a sumptuous and decorative manner so characteristic of 16th century Venice.

With *The Miracle of the Loaves and Fishes* (2), *c.* 1544–1547, by 10 Jacopo Tintoretto (1518–1594) we are already in another era. The High Renaissance emphasis on calm, balanced compositions becomes transformed into a Mannerist concentration on bright surface, excited expressions and elongated figures. The vigorous action of Christ as He hands the bread to St Andrew, and the dynamic movement throughout, point the way to the Baroque.

German painting comes into its own towards the end of the 15th century with Albrecht Dürer (1471–1528), Germany's greatest artist, and one of the dominant personalities of the Renaissance and Reformation. *The Virgin and Child with St Anne* (3), 1519, reveals a perfect blending of the Italian Renaissance style with the German

Gothic. Use of the opposite colours red and green, the abrupt modelling, and vigorous line create a robustness and excitation characteristic of German art even to the present century.

Dürer's contemporary, Lucas Cranach (1472–1553), is credited
9   with having invented the independent full-length portrait. *The Judgment of Paris* (7), *c.* 1528, contains another of his innovations: a
highly erotic standing female nude, fashionably coiffed and bejewel-
led, under the guise of some classical character; here he depicts
Athena, Hera, and Aphrodite – who has just been chosen by Paris
(seated) as the fairest of the three goddesses. In return, she enabled
Paris to abduct Helen, most beautiful of women, from her husband
Menelaus, and thus began the Trojan war. Cranach treats the story,
as well as the nudes, with tongue in cheek.

Hans Holbein the Younger (1497/1498–1543) signed and dated
the excellent *Portrait of a Member of the Wedigh Family* (7) in 1532,
when the sitter was twenty-nine years old. The young man wears
a ring inscribed with the family arms while a paper in the book bears
the motto 'truth breeds hatred,' from the Roman dramatist Terence.

Baroque art was born in Rome in the last decades of the 16th century and grew to maturity during the next hundred and fifty years,
becoming international in scope and spreading to all of Western
Europe.

11   In *The Musicians* (23), *c.* 1593–1595, one of the earliest surviving
paintings by Caravaggio (1573–1610), there is little evidence of the
harsh light effects that would become characteristic of his later works.
The subject may be an allegory for love and music; in any case the
artist leaves little to the imagination concerning his fondness for
langorous youths with red lips and plucked eyebrows. A well-painted
vine in the lower left corner offers an example of Caravaggio's characteristic treatment of still life. Later in the century, Salvator Rosa
(1615–1673) painted the *Portrait of the Artist* (23) wearing a wreath
of cypress, emblem of mourning. The dramatic lighting and the intense expression of the face are characteristics of Rosa that made him
highly revered in the 18th and 19th centuries.

12   *The Fortune Teller* (22), done before 1633, is an early work by the
French painter Georges de La Tour (1593–1652). Unlike his more
famous later works such as the *Repentant Magdalen* in the same room,
where shapes are modelled by the singular light of a candle, he is here
concerned with a daylight scene, and bright reds, whites and yellows
abound.

Nicolas Poussin (1593/1594–1665), one of the most important

11. (left) Caravaggio, *The Musicians, c.* 1593–95
oil on canvas $36\frac{1}{4} \times 46\frac{5}{8}$ in. (92 × 118·3 cm.)
12. (right) Georges de La Tour, *The Fortune Teller,* before 1633
oil on canvas $40\frac{1}{8} \times 48\frac{5}{8}$ in. (101·9 × 123·4 cm.)

artists of the 17th century, is famous both for his landscapes and for great mythological scenes like *The Rape of the Sabine Women* (22), 1632–1634. Poussin's careful study of antique buildings and statuary is evident in the architecture and in the poses of the figures. Another magnificent Poussin is *The Blind Orion Searching for the Rising Sun* (22), 1658, where a classical myth becomes the motive for a heroic landscape. The other great French landscapist is Claude Lorraine (1600–1682) whose *Sunrise, c.* 1647, is a fine work from his mature period, with figures painted by Claude himself and not by others as in some of his landscapes.

The Metropolitan's collection of Flemish and Dutch 17th century painting is outstanding. Frans Hals (1580/1585–1666), achieves his characteristic familiar warmth in *Merry Company* (5), *c.* 1616, where the bright costumes and well-stocked table, painted with Hals' quick open brush strokes, reflect a mood quite different from the sobriety of contemporary Catholic Spain. A radically different mood and technique is to be seen in *The Crucifixion* (17), *c.* 1630, by Hendrick Terbrugghen (1588–1629), a Dutch contemporary of Hals who brought the realism of the early Roman Baroque from Italy. This he combined with a stark Gothicism and a powerful and sophisticated sense of colour to achieve here a deeply emotional religious composition – and at a time when the Netherlands was imbued with a fiercely iconoclastic Protestantism.

The Metropolitan has one of the largest collections of paintings by

Rembrandt (1606–1669) in any museum; two entire galleries are given over to more than 30 works. The most famous is *Aristotle Contemplating the Bust of Homer* (9), *c.* 1635, acquired in 1961 for a price well above two million dollars. Commissioned by Don Antonio Ruffo, a Sicilian aristocrat and man of learning, the picture shows Rembrandt at the height of his creative powers. The aged Aristotle stares with transfixed gaze as he contemplates the bust of the author of the *Odyssey* and the *Iliad,* of whom it was said contained all human knowledge in his head. The powerful mood derives largely from the treatment of light which falls strongly on the lower part of the face. The rest of the painting is either bathed in a quiet half-light or submerged in dark shadow. Rembrandt has exploited the oil medium to its fullest potential – from thick globules to thin colour glazes, thus achieving a full range of expression. From the long chain hangs a medal showing Alexander the Great, Aristotle's pupil, whose own copy of Homer Aristotle annotated. Other great Rembrandts in the collection include *The Gilder Herman Doomer* (9), 1640, *Lady with a Pink* (8), *c.* 1668–1669, from the very last years of the artist's life, and *Man with a Magnifying Glass* (8) which again concentrates on a lighted face that looms out of a subdued background.

A contemporary of Rembrandt and Hals, Gerard Terborch (1617–1681), is considered a Dutch 'little master.' *Curiosity* (16) is characteristic of his quiet interior scenes where great attention is given to the painting of textures. Another 'little master,' Pieter de Hooch (1629–after 1684), like Vermeer whom he must have known, was from Delft. *The Maidservant* (20), *c.* 1670–1675, painted after the artist moved to Amsterdam, recalls Vermeer in its preoccupation with the oblique fall of light through a window to illuminate an interior.

The greatest of the Dutch painters of interiors was Jan Vermeer of Delft (1632–1675). *Young Woman with a Water Jug* (20), *c.* 1664, is perhaps his finest work in the Metropolitan. The composition is perfectly balanced without seeming contrived. Two large areas of blue and red stabilize the composition horizontally and vertically, while it is unified throughout by echoes of blue – in the white headdress, on the wall, and in the shadow of the face and arm of the girl. The *Lady with a Lute* (20), *c.* 1664, in a much lower colour key, again shows a girl by a window, a common subject for Vermeer. The precision of his technique and the sophisticated mood of his scenes become apparent upon comparison with some of his lesser contemporaries in the same room, such as Steen, Metsu, Maes and Ochtervelt. In the same gallery are two fine landscapes, *Wheatfields* by Jacob van Ruisdael (1628/

13. (left) Jan Vermeer of Delft, *Young Woman* with a Water Jug, *c.* 1664
oil on canvas 18×16 in. (45·7×40·6 cm.)
14. (right) Peter Paul Rubens, *Venus and Adonis, c.* 1635
oil on canvas 77½ × 94⅝ in. (196·7 × 240·2 cm.)

1629–1682) and *Entrance to a Village* by his friend and pupil
Meindert Hobbema (1638–1709); the latter is a slight variation on the
scene shown in the two paintings by Hobbema in the Frick Collection.
Wheatfields, from van Ruisdael's mature period, is more romantic in
mood than some of his earlier works.

In 1609, after having spent eight years in Italy in the service of
Vincenzo Gonzaga, Duke of Mantua, Peter Paul Rubens (1577–1640)
returned to Antwerp and to the painters' guild of which he had long
been a member. He married a lawyer's daughter, built a castle for himself, and embarked on one of the most energetic and productive
careers in the history of art. He became the most important painter of
Northern Europe and the greatest exponent of Northern Baroque. His
method of division of labour turned his studio into a factory, allowing
him to fulfill numerous commissions and to realize a very large income.
When compared with artists like Rembrandt and Velasquez, Rubens
may seem somewhat shallow, a decorator rather than a profound
artist, but his art must be viewed in the context in which and for which
it was painted, and with regard to its influence on other artists and
movements. *Venus and Adonis* (18), *c.* 1635, from his late period, 14
possesses an undeniable charm in the splendid facial expressions and
vibrant colours. Rubens depicts the moment at which Adonis, pas-
sionately dissuaded by Venus, who has been accidentally wounded

15. El Greco,
The View of Toledo,
c. 1604–14
oil on canvas
47¾ × 42¾ in.
(121·2 × 108·5 cm.)

by one of Cupid's stray arrows, attempts to depart on the hunt destined to be his last. Virtually unknown until the 1920's, this is one of the few late Rubenses thought to be entirely by the master's own hand. The large *Wolf and Fox Hunt* (18) with all its furious movement exemplifies the type of large vigorous scene that Rubens was often called upon to paint. The small *Triumphal Entry of Henry IV into Paris* (19), *c.* 1631, is an unfinished sketch for one of the large panels commissioned by Henry's queen, Marie de'Medici, after his assassination.

The Metropolitan's collection of Spanish painting, though not numerically large, must be ranked qualitatively above any other in the country, if only for its Grecos and Goyas. The greatest name before Velasquez, of course, was that of Domenikos Theotocopoulos, called El Greco (the Greek) after his birthplace on the island of Crete in 1541.

Cardinal Don Fernando Niño de Guevara (21), *c.* 1598–1600, Grand Inquisitor of the Inquisition, is one of Greco's best known paintings. The Cardinal seems perched on the edge of his chair; his robe juts out in angular points of red: his expression is squirrel-like and nervous. Greco achieves something of the same tense and disquieting mood in *The View of Toledo* (21), *c.* 1604–1614, certainly one of the most famous paintings in the world. Concerned more with expression than with recording fact, the artist creates a dramatic hymn to the city on the Tagus. Buildings are moved and distorted, distances are lengthened or shortened, all in an attempt to heighten the sense of dignity, awe and mystery which characterized this great intellectual and spiritual mecca. Greco's technique of painting wet into wet can be seen to advantage in the clouds above the city where it serves to increase the illusion of movement and mystery. In *The Vision of St John* (21), *c.* 1613, the same technique is used along with striking colour combinations to express the mystical and irrational nature of John's vision. Greco's *Adoration of the Shepherds* and *Christ Healing the Blind Man* are displayed in the same gallery.

One of the greatest Spanish paintings in the Metropolitan is *The Holy Family* (21) by the Valencian José de Ribera (1591–1652) who lived most of his life in Naples. The face of the young Virgin, her hair braided and tied back, her unequivocal glance fixed on the beholder, must stand as one of the clearest statements in the history of art concerning the combined qualities of beauty, intelligence and purity ascribed to Mary.

The Young Virgin (21) is an early work by Francisco de Zurbarán (1598–1664), the greatest Sevillian painter of his time. The strongly pietistic scene shows the child Mary in prayer, surrounded by symbols relating to her piety and foretelling her destiny as the miraculous Mother of Christ. *Christ and the Pilgrims of Emmaus* (5), *c.* 1620, by Diego Velasquez (1599–1660), was painted in Seville before he came to Madrid and entered the service of Philip IV. One is aware of a fascination with strong light effects and differences in texture. The scene depicts the moment after the Resurrection when the Lord is suddenly recognized by two of His disciples whom He has met on the road to Emmaus.

The greatest exponent of the first of the 18th century styles in Italy, the Rococo, was the Venetian Giovanni Battista Tiepolo (1696–1770). He worked in Venice, Germany and Spain where he eventually died. His paintings, along with those of Canaletto and Guardi, will be found in gallery twenty-five on the second floor. The three huge canvases showing scenes from Roman history, *The Triumph of Marius*, *The Capture of Carthage* and *The Battle of Vercellae*, are among the last and most splendid examples of the great Italian tradition of monumental painting. The vigorous movement and dashing colour add to the power of the spectacles.

Several small oil sketches on the same wall were done in preparation for large ceiling decorations. *The Apotheosis of the Spanish Monarchy* is a sketch for the decoration of the Royal Palace in Madrid. The light, airy quality and the radically foreshortened floating figures

had a great influence on the early style of Francisco Goya (1746–
1828) who had come to Madrid from Saragossa in 1776 to work on
cartoons for the Royal Tapestry Manufactory.

    Among his many skills Goya was a sensitive painter of children and
a sympathetic and perceptive painter of animals, as evidenced by his
11 *Don Manuel Osorio de Zuñiga* (13), 1784. The brilliant red of Don
Manuel's suit dominates the painting while the seriousness of his
expression is offset by the three cats who stare hypnotically at the
magpie they must at all costs not devour. The wonderful portrait of
Doña Narcisa Barañana de Goicoechea (30), *c.* 1805, who wears
a ring inscribed with Goya's name is not without its humorous side
either. Doña Narcisa is the epitome of Spanish piquancy. Dressed in
the fashionable 'maja' style (see page 96) she smiles from behind
her enormous crown of ribbons and lace as though about to break
into a giggle. The prominent flower on her prominent bosom is really
a pictorial exclamation point.

    The shift in French art away from the Baroque pomp of the Versailles
court of Louis XIV is signalled by the art of Antoine Watteau (1684–
1721) whose admittance to the French Academy in 1717 as a painter
of *fêtes galantes* marked a major triumph of the *Rubénistes* over the
Poussinistes, and paved the way for the Rococo. His *Mezzetin* (31),
c. 1719, is a painting of one of the stock characters in the popular
commedia dell'arte, a valet and a sentimental lover with a passion for
playing his guitar.

    Along with Watteau, Jean Siméon Chardin (1699–1779) was the
16 most serious of the French painters of the 18th century. *A Boy Blowing Bubbles* (29) may be an allegory, bubbles being symbols of the
transitoriness of human life and the fickleness of women. *The Silver
Tureen* (29), *c.* 1727, is a remarkably well-painted still-life, almost a
tour de force, contrasting the textures of silver, fur, feathers, and fruit
and linking Chardin with the Dutch 17th century.

17   Jacques Louis David (1748–1825) painted *The Death of Socrates*
(30), 1784, about three years after his masterpiece, *The Oath of the
Horatii*, manifesto of the French neoclassical movement. Directly inspired by classical statues and antique Roman bas-relief sculpture, it
is the most important neoclassical painting in America. The story of
Socrates' final hour is told by Plato in his *Phaedo*. The great Greek
philosopher, advocate of natural reason, was condemned to death in
399 B.C. for his pointed criticisms of Athenian society and its institutions. He is shown here in prison, in a heroic attitude, about to
commit suicide by drinking the deadly hemlock juice. At his feet sits

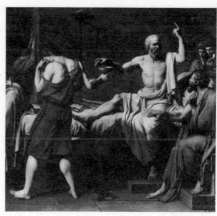

6. (left) Jean Siméon Chardin, *A Boy Blowing Bubbles*
oil on canvas 24 × 24⅞ in. (609 × 63·1 cm.)
7. (right) Jacques Louis David, *The Death of Socrates* (detail), 1784
oil on canvas 51 × 77¼ in. (129·5 × 196·7 cm.)

his great pupil, Plato; Crito is seated with his hands on Socrates' knee, while Apollodorus raises his arms in grief at the right. Painted as it was on the eve of the French Revolution, such an outspoken tribute to a great social and political critic, with specific reference to his self-sacrifice, was itself a revolutionary battle cry. Christian allegorical overtones referring to Christ's Last Supper are also evident, for there are exactly twelve disciples, including three members of Socrates' family, ascending the stairs.

Eighteenth century painting in England is famous for examples of the full-length portrait style begun by Van Dyck in the previous century. Perhaps the most notable in the Metropolitan's collection is *Elizabeth Farren, Countess of Derby* (24), 1790, by Sir Thomas Lawrence (1769–1830), who became painter to the king upon the death of Reynolds. Elizabeth Farren, a famous *comedienne*, married the Earl of Derby who founded the famous Derby horse races the same year the picture was painted. The towering figure, elegantly dressed, with a transitory facial expression, displayed as she is against a moody summer sky, is the epitome of the English 18th century portrait style.

The very mention of 19th century painting immediately evokes the name of France, whose artists and writers played the leading part in creating and defining the various 'isms' of Modern Art. The great

18. (left) Honoré Daumier,
The Third Class Carriage,
c. 1862
oil on canvas
23¾ × 35½ in.
(65·4 × 90·1 cm.)

I. (opposite)
Rembrandt van Ryn
*Aristotle Contemplating
the Bust of Homer*, 1653
oil on canvas
56½ × 53¾ in. (143·5 × 136·5 cm.)

artistic force against which Delacroix' romantic temperament reacted
was Jean Auguste Dominique Ingres (1780–1867), a student of
David, and the greatest exponent of neoclassicism after his master's
death. *Odalisque in Grisaille* (30), 1813–1814, shows Ingres
doctrinaire adherence to essential form, to careful drawing and unbroken line. The exotic portrayal of an odalisque (a Turkish chamber-
maid or harem slave) was a theme taken up by both Ingres and
Delacroix. *Grisaille* is a French word to describe paintings in shades
of grey, often in emulation of sculpture.

In *The Abduction of Rebecca* (33), 1846, by Eugène Delacroix
(1798–1863), the integrity of line is destroyed; everywhere there is
movement and excitement. The mood, heightened by exotic colour
contrasts, violent rhythms and diagonal massing of forms, is as
romantic as Sir Walter Scott's *Ivanhoe* from which the scene is taken.

Honoré Daumier (1808–1879) was one of several Romantic artists
18 who were preoccupied with matters of contemporary life. *The Third
Class Carriage* (33), *c*. 1862, is painted in a technique even more
loose than that of Delacroix. Daumier's concern is not with objective
reality, but with the emotional meaning underlying lonely faces in a
crowded train.

The Metropolitan has a very large collection of the works of
Gustave Courbet (1819–1877). *The Girls of the Village* (35), 1851
is remarkable for the fresh, crisp landscape which was to have a strong
influence on the Impressionists. In spite of Courbet's enthusiasm for
the painting, it met with harsh criticism from those who thought it
realism indecorous, vulgar and disgraceful. The placing of well-
dressed women in the company of cows and a common peasant was
considered a breach of good taste. *The Source* (34), *c*. 1862, shows

Courbet's fidelity to nature and his close approximation to the Impressionist technique in the broken colour of the woods and waterfall. *The* 19 *Woman with a Parrot* (39), 1866, is a frankly sensuous painting which was criticized for its vulgarity, academic emptiness, questionable taste, faulty drawing, etc. It was, however, consistent in its informal pose and unidealized rendering with Courbet's own realism which allowed him to paint nothing he could not see.

Edouard Manet (1832–1883) founded a new style by painting directly from the model using a restricted palette and almost no shading. Basing his art on the examples of Hals, Velasquez and Goya, he remained largely independent of both Realism and Impressionism. *The Guitarist* (39), 1860, an early work which was highly praised by 21 the painter Fantin-Latour and the poet-critic Baudelaire at the Salon of 1866, illustrates Manet's redefinition of the picture plane which was ultimately to save painting from competition with the camera. In all previous painting the canvas served as a window through which the scene was viewed; here the guitarist is on the surface of the canvas itself, integral with it rather than 'behind' it, and the paint is boldly applied in clear, fresh colours. *Mademoiselle Victorine in the Costume of an Espada* (39), 1863, is another of Manet's 'Spanish' subjects. The model is Victorine Meurend, an artist-model who also posed for his *Olympia*, and the famous *Déjeuner sur l'Herbe. The Dead Christ with Angels* (39), 1863, well illustrates Manet's doctrine of 'pure painting' and the autonomy of art. In the 1870's Manet came under the influence of Monet and Berthe Morisot and his *Boating* (40), 1874, reveals elements of Impressionism picked up from them.

The leading member of the Impressionists was Claude Monet (1840–1926), and one of the first Impressionist paintings is his *La Grenouillère* (41), 1869. *Vertheuil* (41), 1880, goes a step further and converts solid mass into a network of colour spots. Monet often painted the same scene at different times of day in order to capture the momentary effects of light. *Rouen Cathedral* (41), 1894, is one of more than thirty versions of the same subject. The great Gothic façade is denied both its monumentality and its permanence as Monet's brush dissects each cubic centimetre of stone into a mirage of colour strokes.

American collectors were among the first to respond favourably to

9. (opposite above) Gustave Courbet, *The Woman with a Parrot,* 1866 oil on canvas 51 × 77 in. (129·5 × 195·5 cm.)
10. (opposite below) Pierre Auguste Renoir, *Madame Charpentier and Her Children,* 1818 oil on canvas 60½ × 74⅞ in. (153·6 × 190·1 cm.)

21. (left) Edouard Manet, *The Guitarist,* 1860
oil on canvas 58 × 45 in. (147·3 × 114·3 cm.)
22. (right) Edgar Degas, *The Rehearsal of the Ballet on the Stage, c.* 1878–79
oil colours freely mixed with turpentine, on paper amounted on canvas
21⅜ × 28¾ in. (54·2 × 73 cm.)

Impressionism, and the fact that the Metropolitan's collection can
rank as one of the largest is due principally to the bequest of Mrs H
O. Havemeyer. By 1929, with the advice of the American Impressionist Mary Cassatt, she had collected works of Courbet, Daumier,
Monet, Degas, and Cézanne, among others.

Pierre Auguste Renoir (1841–1919), deeply in love with life and
beauty, lived a good part of his own life in poverty, and in his old age
was painfully crippled with arthritis. His art, however, shows only a
20 buoyant *joie de vivre. Madame Charpentier and Her Children* (40),
1818, acquired in 1907 at a Paris auction, was one of the first Renoir
to enter an American museum. Mrs Charpentier, the wife of a famous
publisher, is shown seated in her Japanese-style drawing room with
her son Paul (whose godfather was Emile Zola) beside her, and her
daughter Georgette seated on a large dog. The picture is interesting
for its prominent use of black, one of Renoir's favourite colours, and
for the detailed interior foreshadowing Bonnard. Painted at the time
he was beginning to question the narrower aspects of Impressionism.
By the Seashore (40), 1883, shows a close affinity with 18th century
French Rococo. Towards the end of the 1880's Renoir began to
emerge from the harder forms and tight drawing of his 'dry' style
itself a reaction to the looseness of Impressionist brushwork. About
this time he painted *A Young Girl with Daisies* (40), and a few years

ater, *In The Meadow* (40). The latter is remarkable for its structure
and its compositional unity without a consequent loss of lightness
and delicacy.

Edgar Degas (1834–1917) was never completely at one with the
Impressionists, although he shared their interest in light and movement.
His most famous works are pastels of ballet scenes and nudes, of
which the Metropolitan has some of the finest. *The Rehearsal of The* 22
Ballet on The Stage (37), *c.* 1878–1879, is done in a technique known
as *peinture à l'essence* (oil pigment dissolved in distilled turpentine).
Degas shows a characteristic fascination for the effects of glittering
light and rhythmic movement. A slightly different version in pastel
hangs nearby, and a third version is in the Louvre. *Dancers Practising*
at the Bar (37), *c.* 1876–1877, is done in the same technique. While
the painting was in the possession of a friend, Henri Rouart, Degas
wished to take it away and improve it by removing the watering can
in the lower left corner. The story that Rouart then padlocked the
picture to the wall is, however, probably untrue. In 1912, when Mrs
Havemeyer paid over 95,000 dollars for the work – at the time a record
for an Impressionist painting – Degas, seventy-eight years old and half
blind, made the classic remark that he felt like a horse who, having
just won the Grand Prix, gets nothing for his trouble but his oats.

The most influential artist of the last one hundred years is unquestionably Paul Cézanne (1839–1906). By asserting through his
paintings that colour and tone are inseparable, he transformed Impressionism into something solid and enduring. He always sought
the underlying structure and rhythm of forms; thus his art is one of
essences, not of appearances. *Uncle Dominic* (42), *c.* 1866, a bailiff
and Cézanne's uncle on his mother's side, is largely painted with a
palette knife in thick slabs of white, black, pink, and green. The
artist's fascination with the application of paint for its own sake links
him with the Expressionists. *Mont Sainte-Victoire, c.* 1885–1887, is 23
the mountain in Provençe that Cézanne immortalized for the world in
numerous paintings. Already in this early version one is aware that
the real subject is the hidden geometry, the order underlying the
external reality. The landscape progresses from foreground to background in a grid fashion; it is divided near the centre by a single tree
that tends, by its vertical dominance, to draw the foreground and
background together in an almost contradictory manner.

Georges Seurat (1859–1891) also took Impressionism toward
solidity, geometry, and permanence, though by different means than
Cézanne. Pointilism, Divisionism, and Neo-Impressionism are all

23. (left) Paul Cézanne, *Mont Sainte-Victoire*, c. 1885–87
oil on canvas $28\frac{3}{4} \times 32\frac{1}{8}$ in. (73 × 81·5 cm.)
24. (right) Paul Gauguin, *Ia Orana Maria*, 1891
oil on canvas $44\frac{3}{4} \times 34\frac{1}{2}$ in. (113·6 × 87·6 cm.)

terms used to describe Seurat's technique of breaking colours down
into their primary components; e.g.: green into yellow and blue, apply
ing them separately to the canvas so that they will fuse in the retina o
the beholder, thus producing a purer sensation of colour. In *A Sunday
Afternoon at the Grande Jatte* (42), c. 1885, the small dashes o
colour show a desire for order and permanence. They become ever
smaller and more orderly in *La Parade* (42), 1887–1888, lending a
shimmering effect to the stiff, cutout forms. The overall feeling is one
of mysterious stillness, of frozen movement.

One of the boldest advances beyond Impressionism was made by
Paul Gauguin (1848–1903) who at 35 gave up the dubious reward
of working in a Paris brokerage office, later returning to the Islands o
his youth to become the central figure of the Symbolist movement in
24 painting. *Ia Orana Maria* (42), 1891, is the first important painting he
did in Tahiti. The title means 'I hail thee, Mary' and is presumably
spoken by the angel at the left to the Mother who wears a halo, a kind
of re-interpretation of the Annunciation. Gauguin's rejection o
Western artistic tradition, seen in the lack of modelling and perspective
and in the emphasis on colour and pattern, goes hand in hand with
his rejection of Western materialist civilization and his adoption o
'primitive' values and people. *Two Tahitian Women* (42), 1899, from

his second stay in Tahiti, attains a graceful simplicity. The girl on the left is thought to be Pahura, a Tahitian girl with whom Gauguin lived and who bore him two children. Indeed, her face reveals a certain individuality and complexity suggesting that the artist knew her intimately.

One of the briefest, most turbulent and influential careers in the history of art is that of Vincent van Gogh (1853–1890). Born in the Netherlands, the son of a Protestant minister, he was turned out of his job in an art gallery because of his instability. After serving as assistant to a clergyman, he decided to take vows himself, but failed to gain entrance to the University. He lived among poverty-stricken miners in Belgium and later became a vagabond. He left the noise and sophistication of Paris for Arles in Provençe where he nearly killed Gauguin and finally was driven to cut off his own ear. In 1889 he entered the asylum of Saint Paul at Saint-Rémy where he painted some of his greatest works. He rejected Impressionism for a much more subjective, emotional, and expressionistic style well shown in *Cypresses* (42), 1889. From his letters we know these trees obsessed him – he compared them to an Egyptian obelisk. The *Arlésienne* (42), 1888, is an attempt to summarize the qualities of the women of Arles in a single portrait, a kind of concise poetic statement. Much of the flat, poster-like quality derives from the example of Japanese prints in vogue at the time.

Pablo Picasso (b. 1881) was drawn to Paris from Barcelona in 1900 where he shared in the *fin de siècle* discontent that made Gauguin leave and drove Van Gogh mad. *The Blind Man* (43), 1903, from his Blue Period, is an image of acute hunger and loneliness in the Paris streets. The portrait of *Gertrude Stein* (43), 1906, gives evidence of Picasso's nascent interest in Primitive art and Iberian sculpture. In the abstracted planes of the face one feels that Cubism (begun the following year with *Les Demoiselles d'Avignon* in the Museum of 60 Modern Art) is not far away. Miss Stein, a friend of the artist, was both a poet and, with her brother Leo, a pioneer collector of Modern Art.

Modern European sculpture, except for a few pieces distributed throughout the picture galleries, is located around the second floor balcony. It is here that one finds the H. O. Havemeyer collection of bronze sketches of female figures by Edgar Degas, and several fine works by Auguste Rodin (1840–1917), including a replica of his first freestanding figure *Bronze Age*, 1876, which was at one time wrongly thought to have been made from a plaster cast of a living model, so lifelike is its appearance. *The Thinker*, 1879–1889, was originally intended for the lintel of *The Gates of Hell* (inspired by Dante's Inferno) where the brooding figure was to contemplate the panorama of despair below. The inspiration Rodin received from Michelangelo can be felt in the two bronze figures of *Adam and Eve* who seem to grow from the base. Of the smaller works in marble, *The Hand of God* echoes the artist's preoccupation with themes of growth, and *Cupid and Psyche* reveals his love for young bodies in the midst of passion.

A particularly fine work is the slim plaster statue of a young girl entitled *Spring* by Aristide Maillol (1861–1944) whose very different *Torso* is nearby.

Of the several portrait heads by Sir Jacob Epstein (1880–1959), that of the playwright *George Bernard Shaw* is outstanding for the texture of the surface and the rhythm of the modelling.

From the Metropolitan's collection of about 3,500 American oils, watercolours and drawings, only a fraction can be on exhibit at any given time, and only a mere sampling can be treated here. Both American painting and sculpture of the 19th and 20th centuries are shown on the second floor in two galleries beyond Room 8 of the European Paintings; 17th and 18th century paintings can be found in some of the many rooms of the American Wing. A selection of some of the outstanding examples will indicate the wealth of the material which ranges from the austere portraits of early colonial days to 20th century Pop Art.

Smibert's companion portraits of *Francis Brinley* and *Mrs Francis Brinley and Her Infant Son*, painted probably in 1731, are representative of the best portrait style in New England before the advent of Copley and West in the late 1750's. John Smibert (1688–1751) was an energetic Scot who stirred up provincial art circles in Boston when he settled there in 1730, fresh from London and Italy. Three months after his arrival he combined his copies of old masters with his recent portraits of New England patrons into the first art exhibition ever held in America. In his studio he set up plaster casts of antique sculpture as models and taught the Knelleresque portrait manner. *Francis Brinley* is especially interesting for its distant view of Boston which has been called the earliest painted view of that city.

Among Smibert's contemporaries and followers some were European and so, like him, had a fairly sophisticated manner, whereas others, native-born, were primarily house and sign painters or glaziers, like Joseph Badger (1708–1765), who remained basically a primitive. His style is best suited to children, as seen in the charming portrait of his grandson *James Badger*, 1760.

25. Auguste Rodin,
*Orpheus and Eurydice emerging from
the Gates of Hell,* 1893
marble. height 50 in. (127 cm.)

The Museum possesses eight paintings by Benjamin West (1738–1820), all of which were painted in England, where he settled permanently in 1759. In their variety they serve to illustrate the many different styles he adopted throughout his career. *Orlando Furioso,* c. 1793, illustrating the moment when Orlando realizes he has lost Angelica and begins to go mad, is an example of the highly dramatic style and broader brushwork of West's middle years. The beautiful soft reds and blues in *The Wise Men's Offering* are colours that he absorbed from his experience of Venetian painting while travelling in Italy. West played a major role in the development of early American painting through his influence on the crowds of young American artists who visited his studio in London.

John Singleton Copley (1738–1815), reared on the Boston waterfront and largely self-taught, became America's most outstanding painter of the 18th century. He rapidly developed an individual, realistic and direct portrait style, painting an enormous number of affluent New England patrons from about 1758 until the impending Revolution caused his departure for Europe in 1774. His *Midshipman* VIII *Augustus Brine* is probably the finest portrait, and indeed painting, that Copley ever did. It is a perfect example of the softness his portrait style acquired after working for several years in London. Augustus Brine was the son of an Admiral in the British Royal Navy, in which he himself enlisted as a midshipman at the age of twelve, when this picture was painted.

When Gilbert Stuart (1755–1828) returned to America in 1793 with his new portrait style developed from Georgian examples seen during his travels in England, he revolutionized American portrait painting through his immense popularity among mercantile and aristocratic patrons alike. He is most famous for his numerous portraits of *George Washington* of which there are three types – the Vaughan type is the model for the portrait on the present one dollar bill.

The skilled portraits of Thomas Sully (1783–1872) and Samuel F. B. Morse (1791–1872) were the result of a good professional training plus Gilbert Stuart's influence on American portraiture. Sully was exceedingly prolific and very apt at portraying elegant ladies, which made him the most popular portrait painter in Philadelphia from about 1810 till the end of his life. Of the fifteen paintings belonging to the Metropolitan, one may choose his *Queen Victoria* as representative of his genius for capturing likeness and character with rapid brushwork at the height of his career. It is the original oil sketch that he made at Buckingham Palace in 1838, along with other studies.

Morse's *The Muse-Susan Walker Morse*, the artist's daughter, painted around 1835–1837, the years of his invention of the telegraph, has a polish that Stuart never managed to achieve.

Of all American landscape painters of the first half of the 19th century, Thomas Cole (1801–1848) was not only the most gifted, but the most important, for he is usually recognized as the founder of the romantic Hudson River School, the first native tradition in American landscape. *The Oxbow (The Connecticut River near Northampton)*, painted in 1836 after a thunderstorm, captures a moment when the sun bursts through the clouds on to fresh luxuriant vegetation, showing Cole's ability to fuse realistic detail and romantic beauty into a grandiose panorama.

While Cole and his group were inspired by nature, both in America and abroad, other men painted what they saw in the everyday world around them. George Caleb Bingham (1808–1879), the great pioneer American painter of realism, wrote that beauty exists anywhere and everywhere. He recorded vivid scenes of river life, political gatherings, and the Missouri frontier, the most famous of which is *Fur Traders Descending the Missouri*, 1845.

The Hudson River tradition was carried on in the second half of the century by Frederick E. Church (1826–1900), Cole's only pupil, and by the German-born Albert Bierstadt (1830–1902). Church's huge *The Heart of The Andes* of 1859 amazed Londoners, most of whom had never laid eyes on so primeval a view. In New York it was seen by over two thousand spectators in one day at Church's Tenth Street studio, where he showed it dramatically lit by gas lamp in a darkened room. Bierstadt's *The Rocky Mountains*, 1863, measuring about six feet high by ten feet wide, was painted after one of his three extensive expeditions to the Far West, where he sketched all manner of dramatic vistas with Indians and buffalo.

The land and seascapes of Albert Pinkham Ryder (1847–1917) are imbued with a personal and intimate mood of deep intensity and mystery. Ryder was an eccentric recluse and visionary who lived in the private, self-contained world of his imagination. He never dated his paintings, often working on them for years, adding layer upon layer of impasto; but *Toilers of the Sea* and *Moonlight Marine* in the Metropolitian can both be assigned to the 1880's when his work matured, became more imaginative and gained in popularity.

Of the fine selection of paintings by James Abbott McNeill Whistler (1834–1903) in the Metropolitan, his full-length *Portrait of Théodore Duret: Arrangement in Flesh Colour and Black* is the most outstanding. Théodore Duret (1838–1927) was a worldly and elegant French art critic who became a good friend of Whistler after they met in Paris in the early 1860's. Whistler painted his portrait in his Chelsea studio in 1883, signing it with his famous Butterfly symbol; he did no studies, only chalk outlines, and it took him many sittings to finish. He had at first intended it to be a symphony in black, but changed his mind and used colour.

Like Whistler, John Singer Sargent (1856–1925), who was born in Florence and only came to the States when he was twenty, is often considered as belonging to the British School of painting. Sargent was suave, conventional and the darling of the glittering Edwardians whose aristocratic and material splendour is typically personified in his portraits. Moreover, he often ruthlessly penetrated the personalities of his sitters, as in the brilliant *Madame X (Madame Pierre Gautreau)*, 1884, a fashionable Paris beauty, considered by Sargent himself to be his masterpiece although, when exhibited at the Salon of 1884, the decolletage of the black satin dress and the blatant portrayal of Madame's well-known vanity caused a shocked outcry. The Gautreau family asked Sargent to remove it, which he did, keeping the portrait in his studio till 1915, the year before it came to the museum.

Winslow Homer and Thomas Eakins were painters of realism *par excellence*, and Americans are justly proud of their two best-known native artists. Homer (1836–1910) began his career as an illustrator on *Harper's Weekly* in New York, for whom he did his important on-the-spot records of the Civil War: the museum's powerful and sensitively painted *Prisoners from the Front*, done in 1866 from war sketches, brought him recognition as an artist. Homer was not a mystic like Ryder, but a realist like Eakins who painted what he saw, ugly or beautiful, and always with a predilection for the outdoors. From 1883 onwards, when he settled on the rocky Maine coast in a lonely studio overlooking the Atlantic Ocean, he became increasingly absorbed in the sea and its wild moods, translating them into stormy, impressionistic scenes like *Northeaster,* 1895.

26   *The Gulf Stream* is without doubt one of his greatest paintings and certainly the most famous. On trips to the West Indies Homer rejoiced in the beautiful rich blues and greens of the Gulf Stream waters, in the blazing sun and the handsome strength of the West Indian Negroes. Among the many fresh and vivid watercolours of the tropics that show his mastery of the medium is a sketch (now in the Cooper Union Museum) made about 1885 on his first visit to Bermuda; of sharks crowding round a deserted sailboat. In 1899 he put the theme on canvas, showing a small boat dismasted by a tropical squall, with a weary sun-scorched Negro awaiting inevitable destruction from ugly-looking sharks lapping blood round his hull.

Eakins' (1844–1916) realism dealt with people rather than the sea and the forest. He believed that nature could not properly be expressed unless it was scientifically understood; but unfortunately his passionate interest in human anatomy, to the point of requiring his students to dissect corpses, proved too much for the prudish Victorian society of Philadelphia where he lived and worked. *Max Schmitt in a Single Scull,* 1871, was painted during the years when Eakins was teaching at the Pennsylvania Academy in Philadelphia. Schmitt, a famous rower and boyhood friend of Eakins, sits in his scull 'Josie' in the foreground. The artist himself is in the second scull in the middle distance. Eakins left nothing to chance; even the distorted reflections on the rippling water are arrived at logically and mathematically.

The first American painters to revolt against the traditions of Impressionism with its idealistic, sentimental themes, were a group of young newspaper illustrators from Philadelphia: George Luks (1867–1933), William J. Glackens (1870–1938), John Sloan (1871–1951) and Everett Shinn (1876–1953). Together with their teacher and leader, Robert Henri (1865–1929), their work reflected a growing awareness of political and social inequalities which was also being expressed in contemporary writing. Their realism sprung from two vitally new concepts. The first and most significant – as it heralded a dominant theme in 20th century art – was their choice of American city life, both smart and shabby, for subject matter. The second was

26. (left) Winslow Homer, *The Gulf Stream*, 1899
oil on canvas $28\frac{1}{8} \times 49\frac{1}{8}$ in. (71·4 × 124·7 cm.)
27. (right) Robert Henri, *Dutch Girl in White*, 1907
oil on canvas 24 × 20 in. (60·9 × 50·8 cm.)

their style, based on direct observation and inspired by the great realists of the past – Velasquez, Hals, Goya and Manet. In 1908, together with Arthur B. Davies (1862–1928), the modernist Maurice Prendergast (1859–1924) and Ernest Lawson (1873–1939), they called themselves The Eight (the name has stuck) and held their only group show at the Macbeth Gallery in New York. Although public opinion was generally favourable, some critics were hostile and academic artists made remarks like 'apostles of ugliness', 'the revolutionary gang' and, of Prendergast, 'an explosion in a paint factory'. Later they were nicknamed 'The Ashcan School' for their supposedly sordid subject matter.

Robert Henri's *Dutch Girl in White* done in Europe in 1907 and *The* 27 *Masquerade Dress: Portrait of Mrs Robert Henri* of 1911 show his debt to Hals and Manet, particularly in the free and spontaneous handling of the paint. Though Henri's paintings are not disturbing or daring, his earlier street scenes, such as the dark *Paris Night*, 1898, with the waiter standing haughtily distant from a passing lady, and his strong feeling for the texture of paint, were the liberating forces on his young group of students.

Luks, like Hals, was obsessed with characterization. He was something of a character himself; swashbuckling, brash and known to his friends as 'Lusty' Luks. One of his masterpieces, along with *Mrs Gamly* in the Whitney, is *The Old Duchess*, 1905, where he captures with deft, rapid brushwork the individuality of an eccentric old lady in a shapeless hat who wears several dresses at once. Like Luks, Sloan owed his early broad style and dark palette to the teaching of Henri. *Dust Storm, Fifth Avenue*, painted in 1906, shows his genius for capturing the essence of movement and for freezing a moment in time.

Everett Shinn was fascinated by an often false surface glitter of the world of stage performers. In his tiny *London Music Hall* of 1918, the quaint, bowing figure of the performer, spotlit from below and thrown into relief against the darkness of the stage, emphasizes the artificiality of his own presence. Prendergast's *Central Park in 1903* shows a personal transmutation of visual reality into a literal mosaic of glowing colours, achieved through the inspiration of French painters like Cézanne, Bonnard and Vuillard.

The fantasy world created by Arthur Davies' *Unicorns*, 1906, is the farthest remove from the bustling contemporary scenes painted by Shinn, Sloan and Glackens. The scene is enigmatic, filled with soft blues and browns. It is timeless, recalling the pseudo-medieval scenes by Burne-Jones and Dante Gabriel Rossetti.

Though the Eight and their friends liberated representational painting from its academic restrictions, it was the Armory Show that gave Americans their first real taste of Cézanne, Duchamp, Matisse, and Picasso. An atmosphere of acceptance, however, where this new art might take root and grow, was provided by the creative photographer Alfred Stieglitz (1864–1946), whose Photo-Secession gallery, or the '291' as it was called by *habitués*, after its address on Fifth Avenue, became the movement's home base. In 1908 Stieglitz held the first American showing of Rodin's sculpture and drawing; by 1909 he had shown Matisse for the first time in America, and Marin and Maurer for the first time anywhere. During these early years he was constantly showing the works of Manet, Cézanne, Brancusi, and others. One of Stieglitz' greatest contributions to posterity was realized in 1949 when about four hundred and fifty pieces from his collection of American art was turned over to the Metropolitan, making it one of the richest collections of American Modernist masterpieces.

Most of the first American abstract painters were influenced by the Fauves and the Cubists. Arthur Dove (1880–1946) was concerned in his early and late work with the natural shapes of animals merged with their background. *Cow*, 1914, in pastel on linen, and *Goat*, painted some twenty years later, are abstract, but still retain, with lyrical, flowing movement the basic shapes of the animals, which Dove clearly loved. However, in *Portrait of Ralph Dusenberry*, 1924, he departs radically from his usual, still-recognizable forms.

John Marin (1870–1953) had his first one-man show at Stieglitz' '291' gallery in 1909 when he was nearly forty. Probably under the influence of Cézanne and Cubism, he developed an exciting, dynamic style in his numerous watercolours of New York City and the coast of Maine. The Metropolitan has many fine examples. Marin shattered the structures that he saw about him, rearranging them in a kaleidoscope of delicate colours and washes, often leaving blank areas of white paper to set them off. Steel girders and soaring Gothic arches in *Brooklyn Bridge*, 1910, trees in *Tree Forms, Maine*, 1915, and jumbled fields, a church and country houses in *Phippsburg, Maine*, 1932, are only a few of his impressions of an ever-moving, jostling world.

When Marsden Hartley (1877–1943) visited Berlin in 1912 and lived there for the first two years of World War I, he found himself drawn to the heavy, emotional art of German Expressionism. *Portrait of a German Officer* was painted in 1914 in memory of a German friend killed early in the war, and whose initials K.v.F. are in the bottom left corner.

American painting between the two world wars was characterized by a suspension of radical investigations into formal abstraction that had been spurred on by the Armory Show. There was a concentration now on representational painting, on the perfection of technique and on specifically American subject matter.

Artists like Edward Hopper (1882–1967), following in the realistic though less objective traditions of Homer and Eakins, set out to record with precision and gentility their own intimate impressions of American life. The mood in *The Lighthouse at Two Lights*, 1929, and *From Williamsburg Bridge*, 1928, is one of quiet isolation, achieved largely through the use of light, the addition of a solitary human figure in a window merely increasing the feeling of detachment and distance.

In the 1930's a creeping political isolation went hand in hand with an artistic rejection of Europe and of Modern Art in general, with its implied European origins. The radical ideas proceeding from Cubism were now replaced by a dogmatic and chauvinistic adherence to narrowly defined 'American' subject matter and styles. The regionalists, as the group was called, wanted their art to be understood and enjoyed by 'the average American' whom they supposed to be epitomized by the rural Midwesterner. Their spokesman was the critic Thomas Craven, whose invectives often landed harshly on any artist without an Anglo-Saxon surname.

In spite of the narrower aspects of the movement, the paintings of Thomas Hart Benton (b. 1898), John Steuart Curry (1897–1946) and

28. Thomas Hart Benton,
Cotton Pickers, Georgia,
c. 1932
oil and egg tempera on canvas
30 × 35¾ in. (76·2 × 90·8 cm.)

Grant Wood (1892–1941) often achieve more than a mere self-conscious and homespun folksiness. Benton's *Cotton Pickers, Georgia* done about 1932, for instance, shows its debt to Renaissance methods of composition and to the expressive distortions of Vincent van Gogh, to which is added a forceful and imaginative characterization that erupts in the dynamic vitality of plants and trees.

Curry's *John Brown*, 1939, has become a permanent fixture in the visual repertoire of nearly every American. In the mural in Topeka, Kansas – for which this painting is a study – John Brown holds a rifle in one hand and a Bible in the other, thus epitomizing in a melodramatic way the double-edged spirit of the American frontier. John Brown was a violent Kansas slave abolitionist who led the famous raid on the arsenal at Harpers Ferry, Virginia in 1859 in an attempt to free all the slaves in the South.

Grant Wood was born on a farm in Iowa. His *Midnight Ride of Paul Revere*, 1931, painted on composition board, is no less embedded in the popular American imagination than is Curry's *John Brown*. The painting, a reproduction of which, along with Stuart's *George Washington*, hangs on schoolroom walls from Boston to Phoenix recalls the detailed precision of the Northern Gothic painters that Wood so admired during his visits to Germany in the 1920's. The mood, as in Hopper, is achieved largely through the use of light. Paul Revere made his famous ride from Charleston to Lexington, Massachusetts, to warn the colonists of approaching British troops on the night of April 17, 1775.

A regionalist in his middle years, Charles Burchfield (b. 1893) moved away from the qualities of isolation and bleak loneliness seen in his *November Evening*, 1934, to the imaginative vitality and fancy of watercolours like *The Coming of Spring*, 1917–1943, which in its effervescent magical quality conjures up a land that might well be inhabited by Uncle Remus' Brer Rabbit. It was this style in fact that was taken over by Walt Disney for his famous cartoons based on the writings of Joel Chandler Harris (1848–1908). No other American painter has invested nature with the rhythms and cadences of music the way Burchfield has.

Yasuo Kuniyoshi (1893–1953) is well-known for his fanciful and colourful paintings like *Exit*, 1948–1950, rendered in precise, flat colour areas which may reflect his interest in early Italian Renaissance masters such as Giotto and Piero della Francesca.

Lack of formal training has never prevented people from putting paint on canvas, and in the case of Anna Mary Robertson Moses ('Grandma Moses') (1860–1961), it proved a decided advantage. She painted her first picture in 1920 at age sixty and began to paint regularly seven years later. Her *Thanksgiving Turkey* of 1943 recalls her own statement that to her painting was just a pleasant hobby'.

During the past half century the style of painting often referred to as Hard-Edge or Precisionist has attempted to impose a rational order on an increasingly chaotic world of visual phenomena. It was largely the inspiration of Oriental art that helped America's foremost woman painter, Georgia O'Keeffe (b. 1887), to overcome her dependence on three-dimensional realism and to achieve her cool, ordered shapes inspired by natural forms, but transformed, as in *Cow's Skull: Red, White, and Blue*, 1931, by her own personal vision. The painting is a semi-abstract emblem of her beloved northern New Mexico landscape. The shaded planes of the lower half of the skull recall the wind-eroded plateaus and rocky ledges of the Great American Desert.

Charles Demuth (1883–1935) derived much of his inspiration from the man-made shapes of New York City – of buildings, signs and lights. *I Saw the Figure 5 in Gold*, 1928, one of the artist's most im- x portant works, and one of the best known of all modern American paintings, is dedicated to the great American poet and close friend of the artist, William Carlos Williams. The title is taken from Williams' poem 'The Great Figure' which describes the brief and noisy passing through the city of a red firetruck with the figure 5 painted in gold on the door. Through the careful placing and balancing of sharply delineated areas of colour, Demuth creates a powerfully effective evocation of noise and motion which far exceeds Williams' poem as an artistic statement.

Joseph Albers (b. 1888), through his art and through his teaching, has been an important force in American painting for many years. Before coming to the United States, he was both a student and a teacher at the Bauhaus in Germany. He brought with him a detached and highly scientific manner of painting, largely dependent on the physiological effects of colour and form, which has been a major influence on the recent development of Op Art in America. *Homage to the Square: with Rays*, 1959, poses stringent regulations on the artist. He has limited himself to the use of one geometric shape (the square), and to four colours (corresponding to the four sides of the square). The beauty of the work lies in its controlled objectivity, its total lack of reference to anything outside itself — much the way an Egyptian pyramid is beautiful.

American surrealism co-existed with the art of the Regionalists and the Social Realists. It is usually sharp focus, transcribing in minute detail the images of a subjective, unreal world. The fantastic paintings of Ivan Albright (b. 1897), dwell on the morbid aspects of old age, while those of Eugene Berman (b. 1899), such as his *Muse of the Western World*, 1942, are close to Salvador Dali in their dependence on texture and combinations of human, animal and plant forms. Peter Blume (b. 1906), like Berman, was born in Russia. *South of Scranton*, 1931, one of his most famous works, is a fitting together (the artist claims) of visual impressions received during an auto trip from Scranton in Southeastern Pennsylvania to Charleston, South Carolina.

By means of a relentless and frightening repetition, George Tooker (b. 1920) has made his *Government Bureau* of 1956 one of the most poignant condemnations of American bureaucracy. The pervasive theme is sameness, regularity, dehumanized humans who function like the components of a slightly outdated machine.

Andrew Wyeth (b. 1917) stands quite alone — in the midst of an anti-realist artistic environment — as a respected artist working in a tradition of precise realism. *A Crow Flew By*, 1949–1950, one of Wyeth's most popular paintings, is respected by laymen and professionals alike for its brilliant technique and utterly sincere statement without an overdose of technical bravado or a dependence on an underlying 'message'. One may well ignore the pseudo-poetic title which

29. (opposite) Roger van der Weyden, *Christ Appearing to His Mother*, 1440–45 tempera and oil on wood 25 × 15 in. (63·5 × 38·1 cm.)

LS Dᴺ MANVEL OSORIO MANRRIQᵛᵉ D ZVÑIGA Sᵗ Dᴳ GINES NACIO EN 8 AꞮᵉᵉL

ally has nothing to do with the painting itself and which tends to ob-
cure the true subject, which is simply a man named Ben Loper seated
a room with some of his clothes hung on wooden pegs in the wall.

Abstract Expressionism was born in New York in the late 1940's.
s greatest exponent was Jackson Pollock (1912–1956), the most
riginal and influential painter America has produced. His once con-
oversial paintings such as *Autumn Rhythm*, 1950, are in many ways
haracteristic of post World War II America. There is a violent applica-
on of paint with its consequent violent appearance on the canvas.
he influence of atomic theory (invisible forces) and the constant
1ovement of particles of which all matter is composed, sprawling un-
rdered growth, characteristic of the chaotic spread of cities and
uburbs on the American landscape – as Samuel Green has pointed
ut, all this seems to parallel the development of Pollock's art, and to
1ake it a relevant comment on its time.

Thrust by Adolph Gottlieb (b. 1903) derives its powerful effect
om a contrast in shape and function between the two elements of
1e painting, a sphere and a 'burst', as the artist calls it. The two forms
re diametrically opposed to one another; one is formal, static, and
ontained, the other is amorphous, dynamic and sprawling. The ten-
ion set up between the two areas tends to maintain an active balance.

gyptian art is housed in the North Wing of the first floor. The col-
ection is the largest and most comprehensive in America and was
ccumulated over a long period of time. The museum spent nearly
orty years excavating at Lisht and Thebes alone.

A most attractive object from the predynastic period (before 3100
.C.) is a pottery vessel decorated with rows of conventionalized
nimals resembling antelope. From the Old Kingdom (2780–2280
.C.) comes the spectacular tomb of Peryneb, Lord Chamberlain in the
' Dynasty, which was donated by Edward S. Harkness in 1913, and
econstructed inside the museum so that one may actually enter and
iew the paintings and carvings on the inside. These painted reliefs,
s well as those from the *mastaba* chapel of Prince Raemkay (V
)ynasty) are concerned with the daily activities of the deceased. The
urpose was not to depict another world, but rather to show the
nunificence of the present one, and, by inclusion of everyday objects
1 the tomb, to insure its continuance in the next life.

(opposite) Francisco de Goya, *Don Manuel Osorio de Zuñiga*, 1784
l on canvas 50×40 in. (127×101·6 cm.)

30. *Queen Hatshepsut as a Sphinx*
Egyptian, XVIII Dynasty
marble height 64½ in. (163·8 cm.)

Along with the many monumental sculptures of rulers in heavy
stone, the museum possesses several fine examples of Egyptian wood
carving, such as the figures of Mitry and his wife (V Dynasty), the
standing figure of King Senwosret I (XII Dynasty), and the truly re
markable set of funerary models from the tomb of Meketre, an impor
tant noble of the XI Dynasty. This Middle Kingdom set of wooden
figures is the most complete group ever found. The daily activities of
Meketre's estate are depicted in intimate detail, from his yachts to the
cows in his farmyard. Even a superficial look at these intelligent smil
ing faces should dispel any misconception that they were pathetically
concerned with the fatalistic and morbid aspects of death.

From the XII Dynasty also come the grained diorite sphinx statue
of King Senwosret III and the beautiful set of alabaster canopic jars
of the Princess Sithathoryunet. Her pectoral jewel, considered the
finest piece of extant Egyptian jewellery, is inlaid with about 370 pieces
of lapis lazuli, turquoise, carnelian and garnet. There is also a painted
wooden Shawabty-figure (for the deceased's soul to dwell in)
several examples of wooden furniture, and one of the famous blue
faïence hippopotamus figures.

One of the great pieces of New Kingdom sculpture is the huge
30 marble statue of Queen Hatshepsut as a sphinx. (In all, there are 10
sculptures of her.) Easily recognizable in her many portraits, she was
the iron-willed daughter of Thutmose I (XVIII Dynasty) who declared
herself Pharaoh and had her official portraits done in the dress and

ceremonial beard of a man. Upon her death, her son had most of her portraits destroyed.

From the Late Dynastic period there is a fine diorite statue of General Tjayhapme (XXX Dynasty), two enormous diorite sarcophagi, and the famous 'Metternich Stela' which demonstrates the continuing high quality of Egyptian workmanship into later periods. The portrait of a young man, painted on a panel in the enduring technique known as encaustic, where the pigment is mixed in hot wax, is from Fayyum, 2nd century A.D., and is an early example of Egyptian contact with the classical tradition of Greece and Rome.

The large collection of Egyptian smaller arts includes scarabs, gold sandals and headdresses, earrings, rings, brooches, pendants, painted coffins, glaze ware and a bronze coffin for a mummified cat.

A small gallery just off the large hall of Egyptian sculpture contains the Nathan Cummings Collection of Ancient Peruvian Ceramics which has particularly fine examples of two regional styles of Peruvian art: Mochica from the North coast and Paracas from the South. (The exhibit is supplemented with objects on loan from the Textile Museum, Washington, D.C. and the Museum of the American Indian.) Peruvian ceramics are especially notable for their rich designs and deep colours. Much of the figural decoration is concerned with warfare and agriculture, and one is made immediately aware of the high quality of both design and technique. This unity of idea and execution (at the heart of all great art) is well illustrated in the various painted plates and in the small bottle in the shape of a barn owl from northern Peru made about 400 B.C.

The Metropolitan's impressive collection of art from the Ancient Near East is located beyond the Egyptian galleries, at the end of the North Wing on the main floor. (The galleries are presently closed, scheduled to re-open sometime in the future.) The objects range in time from the birth of civilization around 5,000 B.C. to the 7th century A.D. Flanking the entrance to the gallery is a pair of glazed brick lions (6th century B.C.) which once formed part of a passageway built by King Nebuchadnezzar at Babylon (in present-day Iraq). Inside the gallery the earliest ceramics are those from Halicar in southwest Anatolia. The fat fertility-type female figure evolved into a more erect and symmetrical type by the third millennium as seen in a comparison of the two small sculptures in the case opposite the entrance.

A masterpiece of painting in this early period is the large pottery jar from Iran (c. 3100 B.C.) with painted antelope whose enormous horns sweep back over their bodies in graceful curves, proving that sensitivity to design and competence in technique are the heritage and not the invention of the civilized world. One of the most transporting objects is the small gypsum statuette of a votive worshipper from Square Temple at Tell Asmar in Sumer (*c.* 2600 B.C.). The bird like nose and enormous eyes and the momentary attitude of the hand clasped in prayer is one of the clearest evocations of an ancient and mysterious civilization to be found anywhere. A progression from abstraction to naturalism is evident in cylinder seals from the Early Dynastic period. The small diorite statue of Gudea (*c.* 2150 B.C.) Governor of Lagash, shows the ruler in an attitude of worship. Though small in size, the figure is monumental in feeling.

Certainly the most outstanding aspect of the Ancient Near East gallery is the pair of huge stone mythical guardian figures, one a bull the other a lion, with human heads, from the Palace of Ashurnasirpal at Nimrud (883–859 B.C.). Two outstanding works of the second millennium B.C., a copper head of a ruler and a bronze helmet with three figures modelled in gold-silver over a bitumen base, are examples of Elamite (western Iran) workmanship. From the region of the Caucasus and the southern shores of the Caspian Sea come earthenware animals that look like the sculpture of Henry Moore, and fine gold work like the gold gazelle cup of *c.* 900 B.C. From the Achaemenian Empire founded by Cyrus the Great in 539 B.C. there are excellent works in gold and bronze, a beautiful silver pendant in the shape of an antelope, and a bronze ibex head with great curved horns. The newly acquired head of a Sasanian king dates from the late 4th to the early 5th century A.D. It is a true masterpiece of silverwork hammered entirely from one piece.

One can conveniently enter the galleries of Oriental arms and armour from the Egyptian statuary hall on the main floor. Just inside the first gallery is a glass case containing the state scimitar of Murad V, Sultan of Turkey in 1876. The sword, along with its scabbard, encrusted with diamonds, jade, emeralds and crystal is a magnificently gaudy *tour de force*. In the same gallery are examples of Turkish Persian and Indian armour, shields, helmets and jewelled weapons

The collection of European arms and armour is one of the most comprehensive anywhere. The richest part of the collection comes from the period between 1400 and 1800. The main exhibition gallery called the Equestrian Court, houses a brilliant display of armoured horsemen on full-size model horses. From the many excellent pieces in the collection there is room to mention only a few. The earliest work is a Frankish chieftain's helmet of the 6th century A.D. Armour made

elatively early such as the Austrian breast plate of about 1490, and
everal helmets and thigh guards, show the beautiful symmetry and
implicity with which the master armourer shaped and finished his
metal. The museum possesses three sets of armour in varying sizes
vorn by Philip II of Spain at different periods in his life. A large col-
ection of lances, swords and daggers, spurs, helmets, crossbows,
pistols and rifles — through the 19th century — round out the collection
and make it one of the most dramatic in the museum.

Greek and Roman sculpture and painting are displayed in the South
Wing on the first floor, to the left as you enter through the main
entrance on Fifth Avenue. The Greek vases and Etruscan art are in the
same wing on the second floor.

The ancestors of Greek statuary are the many simply-carved figures
from the Cycladic Islands in the Aegean Sea. Dating to the third mil-
ennium B.C., these stiff marble figures are usually of women with their
arms crossed below their breasts and their legs gently separated. They
reveal an understanding of human anatomy that departs sharply from
the older Egyptian formula and anticipates the achievements of Clas-
ical Greece. Two fine examples of Cycladic art are the small statue
of a female, and the harp player, both of the third millennium B.C.

The extensive collection of Cretan sealstones in the style known
as Minoan gives a glimpse of the richness and variety of this art whose
chief masterpieces are to be found in painting and architecture on the
island of Crete itself. Mycenaean art is the early art of the Greek main-
land and is best represented in the museum by painted vases, where
we become immediately aware of the importance of sea-life and
motifs drawn from the sea. It is the Minoan vases, however, which
show a great familiarity with the naturalistic forms of octopuses, due
to the closer contact the Minoans had with the sea.

The next period of Greek art, called Geometric, extends from about
1000–750 B.C. and is well represented by the museum's large col-
ection of vases, the best of which are from Attica, the area surround-
ing the city of Athens. The term 'geometric' refers to the straight lines,
circles and squares which form part of the decoration on the vases
themselves. They are on the second floor and are arranged in three
exhibition rooms, the first containing the early Geometric Vases and
Lekythoi' used during funerals and as tomb monuments. They date
from the 8th century B.C. The scenes which deal largely with battles
and matters of death are thought to represent the very beginning of
narrative in Greek art. The large *Nessos Amphora* is perhaps the
museum's finest example of the style.

The earliest Archaic Greek style is often referred to as 'Orientalizing' because of its incorporation of eastern motifs and techniques. Examples of this style from the mid-8th century to the mid-7th century B.C. are found in the second gallery of vases.

Corinth was the birthplace of the famous Attic Black Figured Vases which correspond to the Archaic style in sculpture and extend to about 500 B.C. In these we see a large advance over the earlier Geometric style; now there are mythological scenes and representation of athletic events. A true narrative art has replaced static scenes and everyday events; costumes and genre are vividly portrayed.

The third room contains the Red Figured Vases from Attica which from about 530 B.C. began to replace all earlier styles. The new technique (a reversal of the black figure technique) allowed a more careful and realistic modelling and is considered the high point of Greek vase painting.

The Etruscan civilization flourished in Italy from the 6th century B.C. and is an historical predecessor to the Roman world. The origins of the race are unknown, though Herodotus tells us they came from Asia Minor, and indeed Etruscan art has an eastern flavour, combining motifs from Greece and the Orient. The objects are to be found on the second floor in a gallery parallel to the one containing the Greek vases. The 6th century winged lion of coarse local stone is a masterpiece of Etruscan carving. A chariot taken from a tomb near Spoleto is decorated with subjects from Greek mythology. A 5th century bronze cista (container for toilet articles) shows the mastery the Etruscans achieved in carving in bronze. In the other three galleries connecting with this one are a large number of Etruscan, Greek and Roman objects in glass, clay, bronze and gold.

If we return to the first floor and enter the gallery containing the Archaic Greek sculpture we can follow the development in three dimensional art which parallels the two-dimensional vase paintings. Roughly corresponding in date to the Black Figured Vases is the remarkable 7th century *Kouros* (youth) from Attica, which once probably stood on the tomb of a young man.

The next gallery brings us to the early Classical period (6th–5th century B.C.). The head of *Harmodios*, a Roman copy of a Greek original, exemplifies the transition from Archaic to Classical. From the height of the Classical period (second half of the 5th century), the age of Perikles, the museum can boast only Roman copies, such as the *Diadoumenos* and the *Wounded Amazon*, which nevertheless show the reserved, dignified, and balanced poses characteristic of what has

1. The Roman Sculpture Hall

ong been considered the greatest period in Western art and has set
he pace for all 'renaissances' since. The greater concern in the 5th
entury for individuality and for momentary poses is well seen in the
ronze *Aphrodite* and in the popular small terracotta figures of women
rom Tangara in Boetia.

This development toward Realism and individuality reached its
ulmination in the Hellenistic period, which is well exemplified by the
nd century B.C. statue of an *Old Market Woman* whose starkly
ealistic features, from her suspended breasts to her sunken eyes, mark
radical change in mood from both the Archaic and Classical sculp-
ures. This same trend is seen in the several portrait heads from the
th to the 2nd century B.C. Examples of Hellenistic gold work include
he famous jewellery from Madytos and the Ganymede jewellery
rom Macedonia.

The long gallery in the centre of the South Wing contains 5th and
th century sculptures from the island of Cyprus. We may single out
he limestone statue of the god *Herakles*, the massive limestone figure
f a votary with archaic smile who carries a cup and a bird, and the
reat limestone sarcophagus with a procession of chariots sculpted
n the sides and what appear to be fertility deities on the ends.

Roman sarcophagi, wall paintings from a villa near Boscoreale, and 31
floor mosaic from a Roman villa at Daphne, along with a large col-
ection of portrait heads ranging in style from the late Republican
eriod to the colossal head of the Emperor Constantine (306–337
.D.) are shown in the gallery of Roman art. One of the most unique
nd popular of the museum's exhibits is the Cubiculum (bedroom)
rom the villa near Boscoreale. Three walls are painted in the illusion-
stic land-and-cityscapes for which Roman wall painting is famous.

The paintings date from about 30–40 B.C.; the mosaic floor pavement, probably from a Roman bath, dates from about the 2nd century A.D.

The Metropolitan has a fine collection of medieval art beginning with objects from the Early Christian period in Rome through the early 16th century in northern Europe. After Constantine removed the capital of the Holy Roman Empire from Rome to Constantinople in the year 330 A.D., two distinct art styles existed side by side, the Byzantine and the Early Christian. This parallel development is illustrated in the museum by the series of exhibits in the two galleries running parallel to the central staircase leading to the second floor.

The north gallery begins the history of western Christian art with a marble fragment of a sarcophagus of the 4th century A.D. It shows children gathering grapes from a vine, illustrating how Christian art was born out of the artistic conventions of Imperial Rome, for the Roman vine has been transformed into a symbol of Christ. The portable objects (largely jewellery) of the barbaric tribes of France and Germany during the 6th–8th century show the dynamic aesthetic of a people constantly on the move. The famous 10th century ivory plaque of the *Virgin Enthroned* is often cited as an example of the Ottonian return to the art of 6th century Byzantium, but it would be difficult to deny the fierce Germanic qualities of the piece which turns the Virgin into a war priestess who wields her sceptre like a club. The agitated drapery reveals something of the same dynamism found in the designs on Frankish belt buckles and brooches.

The south gallery begins with the remarkable 7th century Byzantine silver plates from the island of Cyprus, showing scenes from the life of David and testifying to the excellent workmanship of Byzantine silversmiths. Byzantine jewellery is among the finest in the world and the Metropolitan's collection is superb. Both the plates and the jewellery were found in 1902 at Karavàs, on the island of Cyprus. In this gallery also is a beautiful group of cast bronze Byzantine oil lamps from the 6th century, and fine examples of Byzantine cloisonné enamel and ivory carving.

32   The 12th century marble doorway from San Gemini in Umbria is an excellent example of the Italian Romanesque sculptor's use of classical motifs in a Christian setting.

The Medieval Tapestry Hall contains the beautiful and famous *Annunciation Tapestry* (beginning of the 15th century) possibly designed by Melchior Broederlam, whose art is important as a link between the late Gothic and northern Renaissance styles, and whose *Annunciation* panel in Dijon surely served as the prototype for the

32. Doorway from the Church of San Nicolò
San Gemini, 12th century
marble   height 141 in. (358·1 cm.)

tapestry. The *Rose Tapestries* are 15th century examples either from Arras or Tournai, probably made for Charles VII of France. The *Seven Sacraments Tapestry* is Tournai work from the third quarter of the 15th century. It anticipates the spatial achievements gained through the use of perspective in the early 16th century as seen in the tapestry of the *Fall and Redemption of Man* signed by Jan van Room, a noted Brussels weaver.

Of special interest is a 15th century saddle made of staghorn, entirely carved with scenes of courtship and chivalry. It is probably Italian or German and was presumably used for ceremonies and processions and not in battle.

A small chapel built into the east wall of the gallery contains stone and wood sculptures, capitals and stained glass. An 8th century Italo-Byzantine marble altar frontal shows two symmetrical griffins drinking from a bowl, a motif taken from Eastern art. The stained glass lancet window is mid-13th century, from the former abbey of Saint-Germain-des-Prés in Paris. The scenes tell the story of St Vincent of Saragossa, 3rd century martyr. Of the four wooden madonnas in the chapel, the 12th century one from Auvergne on the right, with its stiff frontality and majestic expression, and the 13th century one from Flanders with the more relaxed Gothic pose, are both excellent examples of their respective schools.

A series of stone heads in the gallery serves to illustrate the qualities of increasing naturalism that accompanied the transition from Romanesque to Gothic.

The greatest examples of medieval sculpture, however, are to be found in the Medieval Sculpture Hall itself. On the wall to the right of the entrance there is a large 12th century wooden Christ on a cross between Mary and John the Evangelist. This type of stiff figure of the living Christ clothed in a tunic was extremely popular in parts of Italy, and especially in Catalonia, in the 12th and early 13th centuries A.D.

A number of madonnas from the 14th and 15th centuries vary greatly in style and quality. The finest example of the 13th century is the small wooden statue in a glass case, heavily over-painted through the years. Of the 14th century is the small *Visitation* in wood poly-chromed and gilded. Of Swiss origin, this group is exceptional for the nearly perfect condition of the paint. The glass ovals on the abdomens of Mary and Elizabeth symbolize their miraculous pregnancies, the reason for their meeting.

In the early 15th century some of the best French sculpture was created by Claus Sluter, court sculptor to the Dukes of Burgundy. The limestone statue of *St John the Baptist* is possibly by Sluter himself for the enormous drapery folds and the realistic expression of the face are characteristic of his style. Two French 16th century limestone statues, one representing the *Education of the Virgin* by her mother, St Anne, the other of *St Barbara* with her tower, are among the finest statues in the museum. The Virgin and St Anne group meets all the requirements of great art, uniting as it does both content and form without any of the insipid mannerism of much sculpture and painting of the period.

There is also a fine sampling of furniture and woodwork, both ecclesiastical and domestic, along with several more tapestries and a variety of minor arts.

The great 17th century iron *reja* (choir screen) which divides the gallery is from the nave of the cathedral of Valladolid, Spain, where it served to separate the laity from the High Altar.

The *Pietà* (in the Treasury) was commissioned (we do not know from whom) by Pons de Gontaut for his château at Biron near Sarlat, central France, in 1495. Pons is shown kneeling on the right, while his brother Armand, Bishop of Sarlat, is allowed to support gently the head of the dead Saviour. The *Lamentation*, also from the château of Biron, and presumably by the same carvers, is the finest sculptural ensemble in the museum. The balance of the figures, their disposition across the plane of the composition, the restrained, contemplative expression of the faces, the gentle movement suggested by the placement of hands and the tilt of heads combine with magnificent skill in carving to produce one of the greatest late Gothic sculptures before he Renaissance in America.

The museum has the finest collection of medieval ivories and enamels in New York. The most famous of the Romanesque ivories s the 12th century leaf of a diptych from Spain showing the *Journey o Emmaus* and the *Noli Me Tangere*. This latter scene, where the Magdalen attempts to embrace Christ after the Resurrection, is one of he most dramatic in all Christian Art, and the 12th century carver has endered it with such dynamism that the movements seem part of a ritual dance. Of the Gothic ivory Madonnas, the 14th century folding riptych showing the Virgin and Child in the centre with two attendant angels on the wings is perhaps the finest. In the case across the room here is a group of small ivory caskets from the 14th and 15th centuries. These boxes were used to contain toilet articles and are decorated with scenes of courtly love and romance often not lacking n frank and bawdy humour.

From the several fine Mosan enamels, we may point to the small Pentecost plaque – part of a set – as one of the best to have survived rom the 12th century. The most unusual example of Limoges work s the large 13th century shrine with cast figures forming a Deposition on the inside. Of rare size and condition, it was unearthed in France n 1896. The bronze-gilt figures were cast separately and then astened to the enamelled surface.

Niello is a mixture of lead, silver, copper and sulphur which is fused nto the engraved lines of a design made on a plate of silver or gold. The small reliquary of St Thomas à Becket is an excellent example of niello work of the third quarter of the 12th century. It was presumably made for John of Salisbury between 1174 and 1176 to contain the blood of the saint, which John had taken from the scene of the martyrdom and later offered to the cathedral of Chartres.

Due to the intrinsic value of precious metals, works from the Middle Ages that have escaped the melting pots of later ages are rare indeed. The popular technique of hammered silver is well exemplified by a 12th century Spanish Crucifix, and by the magnificent 13th century French reliquary head of St Yrieix from a church near Limoges. The parcel-gilt silver of the latter is moulded around a wooden form and backed in place with small wire nails. On the top of the head is a small lid beneath which the relic itself was inserted.

A fine example of parcel-gilt silver work is the 15th century St Christopher from Toulouse with the Christ Child perched upon his shoulder. Other goldsmith work from the late Middle Ages can be seen in the several gold and enamel processional crosses, chalices, monstrances and censers on display at the far end of the Treasury.

Medieval casting techniques usually employed the lost wax process as in the several bronze aquamaniles (water containers) in the shape of real and mythological animals which have a kind of rugged simplicity and durability that differs markedly from the usual preciosity of contemporary works in gold.

One of the most attractive installations in the Metropolitan is the early 16th century Spanish courtyard with its richly carved white marble arcades and columns from the castle of Vélez Blanco, at one time installed in the home of the late George Blumenthal on East 70th Street in Manhattan. Upon Mr Blumenthal's death they were bequeathed to the museum, and in 1964 over 2,000 individual bricks and components were assembled to form three sides of a forecourt to the new Thomas J. Watson library, opened in January of 1965. This is one of the important art reference libraries in the city, presently containing about 155,000 volumes with room for 145,000 more. The books do not circulate, and the library is opened only to graduate students, qualified scholars, museum members and art dealers.

The Renaissance patio incorporates a 16th century Travertine and wrought-iron balcony and below it a 16th century Tuscan marble doorway. The atmosphere of the patio is enhanced by a fountain from the workshop of Donatello which once graced the garden of the Pazzi Palace in Florence.

Through the Tuscan doorway is a small room devoted to the arts of 16th and 17th century Spain. The finest work here is the polychromed wooden statue of *St John the Baptist* by the great Spanish Baroque sculptor Juan Martínez Montañés (1568–1649).

The Metropolitan's collection of Far Eastern Art is so extensive that only a small portion can be on display at any given time; containing over 30,000 pieces in all, it is the largest collection of Oriental art in the country. Several recently opened galleries contain masterpieces of Chinese, Korean, and Japanese scroll paintings, screens, ceramics, jades and bronzes.

The collection of Chinese sculpture is said to be the most important under one roof in the Western World. There is an entire large room containing over twelve monuments of 6th century (Wei Dynasty) sculpture along with the enormous Northern Ch'I Dynasty *Bodhisattva* acquired in 1965. *The Buddhist Pagoda* of the same period, with figures sculpted in high relief on three sides, is one of the most important pieces to have come out of China. It is on long-term loan to the museum.

63. (left) The patio from the Castle of Los Vélez, Vélez Blanco, Almería
Marcael marble (Sierra de Filabres)   height to top of cornice 33 feet (10 metres)
64. (right) A Buddha in the Arthur M. Sackler Gallery of Oriental Art

The huge 14th century (Yüan Dynasty) mural painting from a Buddhist temple covering an entire wall of the gallery is one of the more impressive sights to be seen in New York. The monumentality of the scene (Buddha and his attendants) and the rich colours of the Oriental costumes create a sense of grandeur rarely exceeded by western painting.

In the small sculpture gallery are examples of later Buddhist sculptures in polychromed wood and stone. One T'Ang Dynasty seated Buddha is made of many layers of cloth soaked in lacquer and moulded into shape. A huge bronze Head of Buddha from the Sung Dynasty looks down from a pedestal with half-closed eyes that might well have seen the beginnings of the world.

Examples of metalwork and small bronze sculptures are shown in the Far Eastern Treasury. Ceramics, including the famous Altman and Rockefeller porcelain collections from the 14th–18th centuries, and an important collection of *famille noir*, along with minor arts and Indian sculptures, are shown on the second floor balcony.

Islamic art, the artistic expression of the Moslem peoples, beginning in 622 A.D., is housed in the long gallery adjoining the Chinese

Sculpture Hall. The museum received its first major contribution from Edward C. Moore in the 1890's, and since then its collection has grown into one of the foremost in existence, containing examples of all important mediums and styles.

An excellent example of Seljuk metalwork is the large cast bronze incense burner in the shape of an alert dog, dated 1182, which recalls somewhat the early medieval bronze aquamaniles of the Christian West. From the same period come examples of lustreware pottery which are among the most characteristic and beautiful objects of Islamic manufacture. Carving in ivory is shown to advantage in a small casket dated about the 12th century and decorated with mythological animals carved on the surfaces. Ivories such as this, along with manuscripts, travelled to the West and exercised a profound influence on Romanesque and early Gothic art. Numerous manuscript paintings concerned with religious, secular, and mythological subjects reveal a feeling for delicacy of form and colour unsurpassed anywhere. One of the most beautiful is the Concourse of the Birds, a page from a manuscript of about 1600 from Isfahan.

The height of Islamic ceramic decoration is to be seen in the beautiful prayer niche or 'Mihrab' dated 1354, made in Iran under Mongol rule. Separate pieces of faïence mosaic have been fitted together to form a complex group of designs in brilliant blue, green and white. The collection also contains a group of rare, blue and white, 16th century Turkish pottery, as well as a figurine of a horse and rider from 12th–13th century Iran.

In order to give coherence to the enormous collection of man made objects (with the exception of paintings, prints, arms and armour, and musical instruments) originating in Western Europe from the beginning of the Renaissance to the present day, the museum has created the department of Western European Arts with galleries on the ground and main floors.

The ground floor galleries (about 15 in all) contain exhibits of ceramics, gold and silver work (including the famous jasper and jewelled gold 'Rospigliosi' cup believed to have been made by the 16th century Italian Benvenuto Cellini and now exhibited in the Bache collection on the second floor), along with portrait miniatures, watches and clocks, porcelain, glass, and metalwork. There are also examples of period furniture and some paintings.

On the main floor is a series of more than twenty period rooms completely furnished and decorated, ranging in date from the 15th to the late 18th century, and covering the major styles of Western

:urope. The State Bedroom from the reign of Louis XIV reveals all of he disciplined magnificence of France's Grand Siècle. The great car->et on the floor and the embroidered wall hangings reflect the grandi->quence of the style fostered by Charles Lebrun, the king's first >ainter, who dominated artistic ideas at the time. The room adjoining he bedchamber shows excellent examples of oak panelling and loors from the same period.

The Renaissance in England is represented by a massive and richly arved state bed of oak inlaid with walnut, boxwood, ebony and ash vhich comes from Cumnor Place, Berkshire. This late 16th century nasterpiece of carving is associated with the Earl of Leicester, a avourite of Queen Elizabeth.

.From the Baroque period in England there is an elaborately carved taircase from Cassiobury Park, Hertfordshire, 1677–1680, carved by >ne of England's greatest woodcarvers, Grinling Gibbons, who work-d for Christopher Wren. On the wall beside the staircase is a double >ortrait by Sir Peter Lely, the most important of English 17th century ainters, who succeeded Van Dyck as court painter to Charles II.

The museum's series of 18th century rooms is large and extensive, ne earliest being the bedroom from the Palazzo Sagredo in Venice, vhich is in a style transitional from the heaviness of late Baroque to ne lightness of the Rococo. The rich patterned decoration on walls nd ceiling and over the door are masterpieces of stucco work.

Of only slightly later date is an early 18th century French alcove vith walls of painted and gilded oak panels. The Rococo style is well hown here; all of the furniture dates from the first half of the century, nd the painting of Louis XV as a child-king by Hyacinthe Rigaud, xpresses all the pomp of the era of the 'Sun King'.

The most impressive of the 18th century French architectural instal->tions is the Louis XVI shopfront from No. 3 Quai Bourbon on the Ile 35 e St Louis in Paris, with its delicate wood working and pencil-thin vindow frames. The display shelves are set with fine pieces of Sèvres orcelain, and inside, the walls are covered with watered silk. The rnishings are oak framed, veneered with tulipwood, and inlaid with èvres porcelain plaques; many are signed by Martin Carlin.

The earliest of the 18th century English rooms is the dining room now furnished as a drawing room) from Kirtlington Park, Oxford-hire, c. 1748, which is outstanding for its beautifully decorated :ucco walls and carved wooden mantlepiece and overmantle. The pestry room from Croome Court, Worcestershire was begun in 1763 nd completed in 1771. The walls are covered entirely by unframed,

35. (left) Shop front
from No. 3 Quai Bourbon
Paris, 1774–93
restored oak

36. (opposite)
Parlour from the
Thomas Hart House,
Ipswich, Mass.,
built about 1640

continuous Gobelins tapestry with scenes from Classical mythology
after designs by Boucher. The room was designed by Robert Adam
England's great architect and decorator, whose style may be seen
(without the contradictory Boucher tapestries) in the truly magnificent
dining room from Lansdowne House, London, 1765–1768. This room
reveals the clean, classical lines of Adam's style which replaced the
Rococo as the dominant mode in the second half of the century.

Recently opened rooms include an English room in Elizabethan
style, a 16th century French chapel, a 17th century Swiss room and
two 18th century French rooms.

Notable Western European sculpture on the main floor includes the
small gallery of Italian Renaissance bronzes from the 15th to the 17th
century. The small seated bronze statuette of Paris is by the Mantuan
Alari-Bonacolsi, who was so aware of his position as re-creator of the
glory of ancient Rome that he called himself L'Antico. The gilded hair
makes a striking contrast with the burnished bronze body. There are
also sculptures by Jacopo Sansovino, but the most attractive is the
standing figure of a young negro woman holding a mirror by Sansovino's great pupil, the Venetian Alessandro Vittoria (1525–1608).
Other works are by Andrea Riccio and Giovanni da Bologna.

In the West Lounge are two enormous marble vases made for
Louis XV's royal château at Choisy, one sculpted by Jean-Baptiste
Pigalle in 1745. Four limestone female personifications of the seasons
c. 1730, are thought to be by another great 18th century French
sculptor, Jean Louis Lemoyne. The two long terracotta reliefs and the
lunette by Clodion (1738–1814) are full of the same rococo playful-
ness found in the sculptor's terracotta, The Invention of the Balloon.

'84, located near the Paris shopfront. Jean-Antoine Houdon (1741–
328) was a pupil of Lemoyne and Pigalle, but his style is more
issical, as can be seen in the statue of a *Standing Girl* in the central
illway, and in his *Seated Bather,* 1782, the centre piece of the foun-
in at the top of the stairs on the second floor.

When the American Wing opened as a separate structure in 1924 –
e gift of Mr and Mrs Robert W. de Forest – it presented for the first
ne in an American museum a comprehensive collection of early
nerican domestic and decorative arts in their period settings. On
ree connecting floors, rooms reassembled from colonial houses of
e various Eastern states are arranged in an historical sequence cor-
sponding to three approximate periods of stylistic development,
eriving in turn from the late Gothic tradition, the Renaissance, and
e Classical Revival of the 18th century. In addition to the furnishings
these rooms, the corridors show large supplementary exhibits of
ass, pewter, silver, pottery, and a variety of furniture and paintings.

In passing to the third floor which houses the earliest rooms, one
iould not miss the charming little outside courtyard with its hand-
me marble two-storey façade from the United States Branch Bank,
iginally built on Wall Street in 1822–1824 by Martin Thompson, one
New York's leading Greek Revival architects. The earliest of the
oms is the parlour from Thomas Hart's house at Ipswich, Mas-   36
chusetts, built before 1675. The casement windows with their
ided lights, and the low oak-beamed ceiling and heavy corner-posts
e a survival of the Gothic building tradition brought over by the first
ttlers.

In the 18th century rooms, architectural elements such as moulded

panelling, fluted pilasters and rosettes are evidence of the gradual in
filtration through design books of more fashionable Renaissan
styles. Furnishings include imported luxuries such as a Near Easte
carpet and a brass wall clock, suggesting the increasing prosperity
the settlers in the early years of the century.

On the second floor one wanders through many elaborate mid-18
century rooms with some handsome examples of furniture in the sty
of the influential English cabinet-maker Thomas Chippendale. T
'Pompadour' highboy, *c.* 1795, is an unsurpassed example of t
Chippendale style in Philadelphia, where the highboy, or high che
of drawers reached its most ornate and peculiarly American stage
development. Of particular historical significance is the lar
Assembly Room from Gadsby's Tavern in Alexandria, Virginia. Bu
in 1793, as one of the main coaching-inns on the road to the Sou
this ballroom with its musician's gallery was the scene of Geor
Washington's last birthday celebration in 1798.

On the mezzanine between the second and main floors is t
drawing room of about 1763 from the house of Samuel and Judi
Crommelin Verplanck, which is particularly outstanding because
contains nearly all of its original furnishings. The portraits of Samu
his brother Gulian, and his nine-year-old son Daniel holding a p
squirrel were all painted by John Singleton Copley.

The long Georgian-style hall from the Van Rensselaer manor hou
at Albany, New York, which now forms the west side of the ma
floor courtyard, is a prime example of the rococo opulence whi
rapidly planted itself in Colonial America. The most impressive featu
of the room is its beautiful wallpaper specially painted in London aft
engravings of 18th century French and Italian paintings.

In the early years of the new Republic, rooms grew more spacio
while furniture, following the English neo-classical styles of Heppl
white and Sheraton, became simpler. Among the distinctive inte
pretations of these fashions was the furniture made by the industrio
Scot Duncan Phyfe, who had a shop and warehouse on Fulton Stre
A set of nine matching mahogany side chairs, *c.* 1810, and a state
triple dining table are good examples of his style.

For the visitor who is interested in early American silver, the displ
on the main floor offers a wide selection of works by New York a
New England silversmiths, including some pieces by the famous Pa
Revere of Boston (1735–1818).

Henry William Stiegel came to America from Cologne in 1750. I
1765 he had founded a glass furnace at Mannheim, Pennsylvan

ere he employed skilled blowers to produce quantities of table and
usehold glass. The corridors of the second and main floors contain
e examples of small pitchers, bottles, and moulded sugar bowls in
1, clear amber, bright blue, green and amethyst from the Frederick
 Hunter collection of Stiegel glass.

The colourful crafts of the Pennsylvania Germans are the most
ginal and distinctive of all American folk arts. Seeking political and
gious freedom, these settlers from the Rhineland and Palatinate
ions of Germany established a local artistic tradition which
urished from 1750 to 1850, and can still occasionally be found in
 Pennsylvania Dutch Country today. The exhibits arranged near
 main floor entrance to the American Wing all belong to a native
asant art brought from the Old World.

The collection of musical instruments numbers nearly 4,000
ects, and includes instruments from pre-history, ancient Egypt,
ope, Africa, Asia, Oceania and America. Highlights of the col-
tion include the first pianoforte, 1720, built in Florence by Barto-
imeo Cristofori; the earliest double virginal known, built in
twerp in 1581; a spinetto made in Venice in 1540 for the Duchess
Urbino; and three violins from the shop of Antonius Stradivarius.

The Costume Institute of the Metropolitan Museum offers exhibits
signed to show the social, technical, and aesthetic values of
stume. The collection is international in scope, includes thousands
tems and spans four centuries in date.

The Junior Museum holds excellent exhibitions on art and archaeo-
y for children. There are buttons to push, recorded talks to listen to,
d colourful and informative displays.

On the south wing of the main floor is a large, cafeteria-style
taurant. It is open Monday through Saturday, 11 a.m.–2.30 p.m.;
ndays 12 p.m.–3 p.m. Coffee alone is served on Saturdays from
.m.–4.30 p.m. and Sundays from 3.30 p.m.–4.30 p.m.

On the main floor, near the Fifth Avenue entrance, a well-stocked
ok store sells books, post cards, slides, reproductions, and high
ality gifts and facsimilies of objects in the museum collections.

Special events include concerts, films, lectures and Acoustiguide
rs. Arrangements must be made in advance for personally guided
rs.

The Director of the Museum is Mr Thomas Hoving.

The Metropolitan is open: Monday, Wednesday, Thursday, Friday,
 a.m. to 5 p.m.; Tuesday, 10 a.m.–10 p.m.; Sundays and holidays,
.m.–5 p.m.

The Cloisters

Fort Tryon Park
Madison Avenue Bus 4 to door; IND Subway (Eighth Avenue) 190th
Street Station

37 The Cloisters is perhaps New York's most unique museum a
certainly its most beautiful. Located at the extreme northern tip
Manhattan Island with a breathtaking view of the Hudson River a
the Palisades, unlike most museums, the Cloisters is not merely
building with paintings hung on walls. By incorporating elements
medieval architecture and sculpture in the actual structure of
museum building itself, a rare feat was accomplished: the constructi
of a museum of medieval art in which all media (sculpture, arc
tecture, painting) are represented and combined to form a harmonic
whole.

The Cloisters came into being in 1926 when the Metropolit
Museum of Art, with funds donated by John D. Rockefeller, Jr, p
chased the collection of sculpture and architectural elements belor
ing to the American sculptor George Grey Barnard. Mr Rockefe
presented a number of additions to the collection, and in 1930 he g
the land overlooking the Hudson River, now Fort Tryon Park.

The design and construction of the building was entrusted to
firm of Allen, Collens and Willis of Boston, under the direction
Joseph Breck, then Assistant Director of the Metropolitan. La
James J. Rorimer saw the work to completion and became the n
director of the Cloisters.

As far as possible, an attempt was made to recreate the plan c
12th century Romanesque monastery similar to that of San Michel
Cuxa in the French Pyrenees, but no single monument was cop
exactly. An effort was also made to make obvious what is authentic
ly medieval and what is modern, so that the visitor should have
trouble identifying the original architecture. The collection includ
works of Western European Christian art, mostly from the 12th to
early 16th century, in all media.

To the medieval craftsman, all things were a reflection of Div
presence; the modern distinction between function and beauty
not exist. Manufacture was a religious act, a metaphor for the Creati
The end of the artist's work was directed toward the glorification

d, and he therefore had every reason to care intensely about what
made and how well he made it. Every book, chair, retable, and
ital in the museum is a testimony to this fact.

By way of introduction to the periods covered, the three doorways
the Romanesque Hall serve to illustrate the transition from
manesque to Gothic which unfolds as one travels through the
seum. The entrance doorway, probably from Poitou in France,
1-12th century, is a good example of the sturdy Romanesque man-
, with its semi-circular arch placed on heavy columns. The out-
nding decoration is to be found at the three most important points
he arch, the keystone and the capitals. About 150 years later is the
orway from Reugny in the upper Loire Valley which is in a transi-
nal style. The slightly pointed arch and cusped archivolt remind one
he eastern styles that were an important influence in the formation
the Gothic. The doorway from the ancient monastery of Moutiers-
nt-Jean in Burgundy is 13th century and fully Gothic in its rich
d elaborate decoration. The sculptured figures of Clovis and his son
othair on the left and right jambs respectively are in celebration of
legend that relates how Clovis, the first of the Merovingian kings

(left) The Cloisters showing windows from Sens and from Froville arcade
(right) The Apse from the church of San Martin
untidueña, Segovia, Spain, 12th century

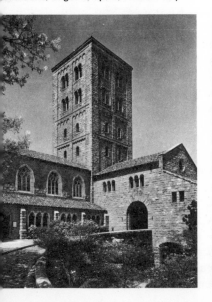

of France, donated to the monastery as much land as could be e
circled in one day by a man riding an ass.

The variety within the style we call Romanesque becomes appare
when we compare the columns and capitals from the lovely, ligh
filled cloister of Saint-Guilhem-le-Désert with the Cuxa Cloist
located on opposite sides of the Romanesque Hall. The beauti
acanthus leaves of the Saint-Guilhem capitals are the work of
extremely competent and sensitive stone carver, for the forms tw
and bend in a manner reminiscent of living vegetation. The soft lim
stone found in the south of France allows for freer handling than t
hard pink marble of the Pyrenees that we find in the Cuxa Cloist
The sculptor of the Saint-Guilhem capitals, probably under the i
spiration of visible monuments from the Roman period, allows for
to overlap, and creates deep cuts in order to effect a maximum e
ploitation of the shadows created by the bright sunlight of Proven
The Cuxa sculptor, on the other hand, had not the amount of Rom
columns and capitals to inspire him, nor could he make use of brig
sunlight. His marble, however, was of itself so colourful that, as hea
as the columns are, we still derive a sense of lightness from the cloist

38   The largest and most impressive piece of original architecture
the Cloisters is the Romanesque Apse from the church of San Mart
in Fuentidueña, Segovia, Spain. It is on indefinite loan from the Spa
ish government. Under the direction of Miss Carmen Gómez-More
of the Metropolitan's Medieval department, the apse was pain
takingly dismantled in Spain, then shipped stone by stone to Ne
York where it was carefully reconstructed. The original church w
built about 1160 and dedicated to St Martin of Tours, one of the mo
popular saints of the time. There are many representations in mediev
art of St Martin dividing his cloak with the beggar. He is shown he
to the left of the apse, in his role as Bishop.

In the semi-dome of the apse (which is the easternmost end of t
church and corresponds to the dome of Heaven) is a fresco remov
from the church of San Juan de Trédos in the Catalan Pyrenees. T
scene represented is *The Adoration of the Magi* and when we rec
that the Adoration took place only a short time after the birth
Christ, we may wonder why Jesus is shown as a young boy. T
answer lies at the very heart of the painting; the Trédos fresco is r
narrative, but iconic. The scene does not take place in historical tim
the Virgin and Child are separated from the Magi by an almo
shaped, multi-coloured band called a mandorla, a symbol of divini
The mandorla destroys time sequences; the past, present and futu

39. (left) *Ivory Cross* (reverse), second half of the 12th century; English
walrus ivory   height 22⅝ in. (57·3 cm.)
40. (right) *St Catherine Tended by Angels* from *Les Belles Heures*
of Jean, Duke of Berry, *c.* 1410–13 vellum

become fused in religious symbol. Both Christ and Mary are the
epitome of timeless being and Divine Majesty as they sit erect, staring
from the 'dome of heaven.'

The technique used in the Trédos painting is known as *buon
fresco,* which means that the pigments were painted directly on the
wet lime mortar of the wall, forming a strong chemical bond. The
paintings from San Baudelio de Berlanga are done in *fresco secco,* a
less permanent technique where the plaster is largely dry at the time
of painting and the pigment is applied *on* rather than *into* the wall. All
of the frescoes at the Cloisters have been transferred to canvas in
order to preserve them.

In the centre of the chapel is the now famous Ivory Cross thought 39
to have originated from the monastery of Bury St Edmunds in Suffolk,
England. A true masterpiece of Romanesque ivory carving, the cross is
completely carved on front and back with one hundred and eight
figures and more than sixty inscriptions both in Latin and Greek. A
close look at the cross reveals that none of the three main sections
are perfectly straight. These are the natural curves of the walrus

tusk from which the pieces are carved, though the artist has done ;
remarkable job of compensating for irregularities by shaping th'
pieces and fitting them together in a masterly manner. The theme o
the representations is *The Passion of Christ*, the events of *Chris*
before Pilate, The Deposition, The Three Maries at the Tomb, an·
The Ascension being represented on the base and terminals in minut
detail. *The Crucifixion* itself would have been represented by ;
(probably bronze) figure of Christ fixed to the face of the cross witI
ivory pegs. On the reverse are the four symbols of the Evangelists
Matthew, Mark, Luke and John (Matthew is missing from the base)
The Piercing of the Lamb of God, symbolic of the sacrifice of th·
Crucifixion is in the centre. The two curious figures at the base of th
front of the cross are Adam and Eve who were believed to have bee·
resurrected on the day of the Crucifixion.

The panels of stained glass in the Langon Chapel are of the 13tI
century and are believed to have come from a church in Troyes, o·
the river Seine. The 13th was a great century for stained glass, an·
the colours, especially the rich cobalt blue, have defied attempts a
reproduction ever since. Stained glass is made by mixing the oxide
of various metals with molten glass. The glass is then rolled into ;
plate, cut into suitable shapes and fitted between grooved strips o
lead. The finer details of face and costume are often added by brush

The seated *Virgin and Child* on the altar in the Langon Chapel wa·
carved from a single block of birch wood, and is among the fines
Romanesque wood sculptures in the United States. At one time com
pletely gessoed and polychromed in bright blue, green and red, th·
Virgin still retains one of her jet eyes. Somewhat less rigid than th·
Trédos Virgin, she glances slightly to her right as a gentle smile rest·
on her lips and a tiny mysterious breeze lifts a corner of her robe.

Little more than a hundred years later, an entirely different set o
influences converged in Strasbourg on the river Rhine to produce ;
style exemplified by one of the most beautiful early Gothic sculpture·
to have crossed the Atlantic Ocean, the *Strasbourg Virgin* in the Earl
Gothic Hall. All of the stiff, hieratic and 'primitive' qualities o
Romanesque art have vanished. There are deep folds in the drapery
handled not like limestone, but clay; the horizontal and vertical balanc·
of one part against another is in perfect harmony with the whole
Even the personality of the Virgin becomes tangible. She is neither ;
transcendent image of divinity nor, as in later Gothic sculptures in th·
same room, a coquettish lady of fashion.

On the lower level of the building, adjoining the Glass Gallery i·

he early 14th century cloister from the abbey of Bonnefont-en-Comminges in south-central France. During the 19th century most of he capitals, shafts and sculptures from Bonnefont were dispersed and oday the monastery is in ruins. The Herb Garden which the cloister rames is a unique attraction, for it is one of the few medieval herb jardens in existence. It was suggested by medieval manuscripts and panel paintings and contains many of the important plants depicted n the *Unicorn Tapestries* and other works of art. With its excellent view of the famous George Washington Bridge and the Hudson River, his tiny corner of Manhattan Island is certainly one of the most beautiful spots on a warm spring day. The cloister adjoining the garden on the east is from the 15th century convent of Trie near Toulouse.

Later Gothic sculpture and 15th century German painted glass roundels are exhibited in the Glass Gallery at the end of which is an altarpiece of the *Nativity and Vision of the Magi* by a 15th century ollower of Roger van der Weyden.

The Treasury is graced by the presence of the much-discussed *Antioch Chalice,* once imagined to be the Holy Grail itself. The chalice s reputed to have been found in a well by some Arab workmen in Antioch in 1910. It is the earliest object in the museum, belonging chronologically and stylistically to the first period of Christian art, known as Early Christian. The decoration on the outside of the chalice s silver (once gilded) showing Christ (twice represented) seated with His apostles among the symbolic grape vines. We have a perfect example here of nascent Christian art adopting the artistic vocabulary of Imperial Rome to its own symbolic uses. The vine, the lamb, and he seated figures wearing togas are all commonplace in Roman art, but here they assume a new role and become symbols not of the Bacchic rite, but of the Christian faith. The vine recalls Christ's words n the Gospel of St John: 'I am the true vine, and my father is the husbandman; I am the vine, ye are the branches.'

Of the many liturgical objects in the Treasury, the *Bertinus Chalice* s a fine example of 13th century jewellers' work. The beautiful lightly hammered appearance of the gold gives the surface a vitality which is offset by the tasteful monumentality of the design.

One of the best pieces of Limoges enamel in the Treasury is the small *Eucharistic Dove* of the 13th century. A container for the Host which fits inside the lid on the back, it was suspended above the altar o be seen when no service was in progress. Some of the most original of medieval liturgical objects are the several cast bronze *aquamanile* n the shapes of various real and mythological animals which were used by the priest to wash his hands.

The cult of sacred relics was important from the 4th century, and in the latter Middle Ages churches and monasteries collected great quantities, often engaging in fierce and sometimes none too ethical competition with regard to which church had the *real* relic of this or that saint. Relics were invested with certain magical powers which drew large numbers of people on pilgrimages. Being infinitely prec- ious objects, they were kept in appropriate dwelling places which often took the form of that part of the body they housed; thus we find reliquaries in the shape of heads, arms, legs, fingers and feet. The reliquary statue of St Stephen is an important example of Mosan goldsmith work. The style is close to that of Nicholas of Verdun, greatest of Romanesque goldsmiths.

One of the most bizarre reliquaries is the moulded leather shoe which once probably held the right foot bone of St Margaret of Antioch who is shown in numerous medieval representations with her right foot on the neck of a bulging-eyed devil. Legend has it that when the devil tempted Margaret she threw him to the ground and put her right foot on his neck saying: 'Lie still, thou fiend under the foot of a woman'. The piece is thought to be 14th century French.

Among the Cloisters' most treasured possessions are two books of 40 hours: *Les Belles Heures* of Jean, Duke of Berry and Prince of France, and the *Hours of Jeanne d'Evreux*, wife of Charles IV of France. The smaller of the two is the earlier. The workmanship, incredibly fine and detailed, is that of Jean Pucelle, greatest Parisian miniaturist of the 14th century, who exercised a profound influence on the entire his- tory of art by introducing the innovations of Giotto and Duccio from Italy into the North. The book of hours was an abbreviated version of the clergy's own service books. Designed for private worship, it traditionally consisted of a calendar as a guide to feasts and saints' days, readings from the Gospels, the Office of the Virgin, the Office of the Dead, the Penitential Psalms, and the Litany of the Saints. One may well wonder at all the curious goings on in the margins of a book designed for prayer, but the various exotic animals, troupes of soldiers, monkeys, dogs, lions, musicians and beggars, known as *drôleries*, which means 'funnies', are part of an old and venerable tradition in Northern art. They are a sort of pictorial counterpart to late Medieval Mystery Plays which became increasingly filled with bold spectacle and secular allegory.

The larger book is believed to have been illuminated by Pol de Limbourg and his brothers, who painted the famous *Très Riches*

Heures, now in Chantilly. The manuscript was made during the first decade of the 15th century and is one of the finest expressions of French courtly art in the late Gothic period, before the invention of the printing press.

In a room at the top of the stairs leading from the Glass Gallery hang the famous *Unicorn Tapestries.* All but two are believed to have III been woven for Anne of Brittany (1476–1514) in celebration of her marriage to Louis XII (1462–1515) on January 9, 1499. For many generations they were in the possession of the Rochefoucauld family, then during the French Revolution they were removed from the castle, and according to one account were used to keep potatoes from freezing. They were recovered by the Rochefoucaulds in the 19th century, remaining with them until they were purchased by John D. Rockefeller in 1920, and later donated by him to the Cloisters.

The tapestries are remarkable for their wealth of detail, brilliant colours and nearly pristine state of preservation. One could hardly ask for a more authentic document of 15th century French courtly life, illustrating the taste and temper of the times and revealing the close connection between a variety of prevalent themes in art and literature: the hunt, mythical and Christian allegory, pageantry and courtly love, combined with the realistic treatment of faces, flowers and plants, and employing the recent achievements in aerial and linear perspective. Most remarkable of all is that such a fusion should occur in so difficult a medium as tapestry weaving.

The unicorn is a mythological animal which is described in ancient Greek literature and appears in the folklore of India and the Near East. In the Christian Middle Ages it came to symbolize virility, virginity and purity. Legend tells us the unicorn is such a swift animal that it may not be captured by hunters, but only by a trick. In the first tapestry of the series, made somewhat later than the others, the royal hunting party sets out with dogs and spears in search of the unicorn. The initials A E, seen throughout the series and tied together with a gold cord, are the first and last letters of Anne's name and the first and last letters of her motto, *'à ma vie'.* They are tied together with her device, a *cordelière,* which derives from the cords used by the Franciscans to tie their habits. Anne founded the chivalric order of the Dames of the Cordelière, and the convent of that name in Lyon was built at her request.

The second tapestry in the series and the first actually made for III Anne shows the hunting party gathered around a fountain, not far from the royal castle. The unicorn plunges his horn into the stream in a symbolic gesture to draw the poison from the water before the animals take a first drink in the morning. By thus taking poison and suffering on himself, the unicorn becomes a symbol of Christian sacrifice and martyrdom. His horn was thought to have purgative powers and was valued highly as an object of semi-religious veneration. In the third tapestry the unicorn makes a dash for his freedom but is surrounded by spear points; the first wound has been inflicted. In the fourth tapestry he kicks at his pursuers and lacerates a hound's side with his horn. In the fifth, a hunter is about to sound his horn but is hushed by an attendant lady while the unicorn approaches the maiden whose hand we see guiding him by the neck. Unfortunately, the actual capture of the unicorn in the maiden's lap is lost, but in the sixth tapestry the slain animal is brought before the king and queen, draped over the back of a horse. The last of the series was made somewhat later than the others. It shows the unicorn sitting inside a small, round, fenced enclosure on a *millefleurs* background. He wears a brightly decorated collar with a gold chain attached to a pomegranate tree.

The Spanish room is so named after its beautiful and rare 15th century Castilian Gothic Painted Ceiling which is said to have come from a bedroom once occupied by Francis I of France while he was a 41 prisoner of Charles V. The room houses the famous *Mérode Altarpiece*, one of the most important early Flemish paintings in America. It was acquired by the Cloisters after it had been in the possession of the Mérode family for more than two generations. The central panel of the triptych shows the *Annunciation;* in the left wing are the donors, while the right wing shows St Joseph in his carpenter's shop. The painting was probably executed about 1425, some six years earlier than the famous Ghent altarpiece by the brothers Van Eyck. The artist who painted the *Mérode Altarpiece*, tentatively identified as one Robert Campin, teacher of the great Roger van der Weyden, is an early exponent of a tradition of realism quite opposed to the preciosity of the Van Eycks. Campin's plump annunciate is seated on the floor of a modest bourgeois livingroom, and not on the porch of the traditional Gothic church. A certain love for humble things and for the surfaces and textures of everyday objects in common use can be seen especially in the St Joseph wing. This exhaltation of the value of honest labour, in sharp contradiction to the excesses of certain elements of the aristocracy and ecclesiastical hierarchy, would culminate a hundred years later in the Protestant Reformation.

Even the 'newest' innovations, however, are not divorced from tradition, and the new interest in realism had to come to terms with a

41. Robert Campin, *The Mérode Altarpiece, c.* 1425
tempera and oil on wood central panel 25¼ × 24⅞ in.
(64·1 × 63·1 cm.) left wing 25½ × 10¾ in.
(64·7 × 27·3 cm.) right wing 25½ × 10⅞ in.
(64·7 × 27·6 cm.)

tradition of symbolic representation as old as Christianity itself. The result is one of the most realistic as well as theologically complex paintings of its period. With the exception of the angel's wings and the tiny Christ Child with the cross, there is nothing in the painting that could not stand the scrutiny of the most sceptical logical positivist. All the objects, the laver, the towel, the candles, the lilies, the mouse-trap on Joseph's workbench, are perfectly convincing as real objects of everyday use. The symbolism has become disguised, the objects are now metaphors for things divine. The lily, laver and towel symbolize Mary's purity; the extinguished candle on the table went out in the overwhelming presence of divine light entering with Jesus through the window; the mousetrap is thought to symbolize God's having tricked and 'caught' the Devil through the Crucifixion and the Resurrection.

The Executive Assistant in charge at the Cloisters is Thomas P. Miller.

Numerous publications on objects in the Cloisters' Collection, including an excellent paperback guide, are available at the sales desk. The museum is opened from 10 a.m. to 5 p.m. Tuesdays through Saturdays and from 1 p.m. to 5 p.m. on Sundays and holidays. It is closed Mondays.

The Frick Collection

One East 70th Street
IRT Subway (Lexington Avenue) 68th Street Station

42 The Frick Collection contains paintings, sculpture, drawings, enamels, bronzes and furniture once belonging to the Pittsburg Coke and Steel industrialist, Henry Clay Frick (1849–1919). One of the few museums which always was, and still is, a private residence, the mansion was built for Mr Frick in 1913–1914 in the late 18th century French Neo-Classic style of Louis XVI by the American architect Thomas Hastings. Of some forty rooms in the entire house, only about fifteen on the first floor are open to the public. After the death of Mrs Frick in 1931, the building and the collection it housed were left to a board of trustees in order to serve the advancement of the fine arts. Following some alterations in 1935, it was opened as a museum. The Frick Art Reference Library (entrance on 71st Street) is open to graduate students and other interested adults. It contains the finest private collection in America of books and photographs pertaining to the fine arts.

The collection is strongest in 17th–18th century French, Dutch and English painting, Italian Renaissance painting and bronzes, and 16th century Limoges enamels. A few selected works from other periods are also shown. From time to time paintings may be moved or taken off view, but for the most part the exhibitions can be considered permanent. The paintings are not arranged in chronological order and the most advantageous way to see the collection is to follow the itinerary suggested in the small leaflet sold for ten cents in the lobby.

The South Hall contains two paintings by Jan Vermeer, *An Officer and a Laughing Girl* of about 1656 and *Girl at Her Music*, about 1660. In the earlier painting, the illusion of objects and persons disposed in space is achieved largely by light and not lines. A single light source (from the open window) illumines surfaces from a particular point, creating an illusion of intimacy as we eavesdrop from the foreground shadows. Vermeer's interest in light and the appearance it lends to objects can be seen in the intricate reflections from the window glass and from the drinking-glass held by the girl.

The *Coronation of the Virgin* is the latest known work by the founder of the Venetian school of painting in the trecento, Paolo Veneziano

42. The Frick Collection

active 1333–1358), who was instrumental in moving away from the formal abstraction of the Byzantine school to a more natural and sensual aesthetic so characteristic of later Venetian painting. The dogma of the Virgin as Queen was established in the 5th century, but the theme of Christ crowning her did not become popular until about 1250. The scene as here portrayed represents not only the supreme event in the life of the Virgin, but is also to be understood as an exhaltation of Mary as the personification of the Church.

On the other side of the hall hangs Boucher's small painting of his wife reclining on a divan, signed and dated 1743. She was 27 at the time, had been married for 10 years, and was the mother of three children, two of whom married famous artists. The treatment is spontaneous, informal and full of rococo sensuality. The *Mother and Children* by Renoir, who died in the same year as Mr Frick, was purchased by him in 1915. The immediacy and freshness of the treatment remind us of Renoir's fondness for young women and children as subjects, and the broken strokes of colour place the date about 1875, before the artist emerged from his Impressionist phase.

The eight rectangular canvas panels with allegorical representations of the *Pursuits of Man* by François Boucher (1703–1770), in the room bearing his name, were painted for Madame de Pompadour (1721–1764), mistress of Louis XV, for the boudoir of her château at Crécy. They were acquired in 1916 and installed in Mrs Frick's second floor bedroom which has now been transplanted to the main floor with all eight panels on public display. Full of grace, delicacy and provocative charm, the series is one of the finest done in the 18th century.

Nor are the themes as frivolous as they might at first seem, for the idea
of children aping the pursuits of adults is satiric in intent, and ultimately
an appeal to the predominately rational mind of the age.

The Dining Room contains 18th century English paintings by
William Hogarth (1697–1764), Sir Joshua Reynolds (1723–1792),
Thomas Gainsborough (1727–1788), George Romney (1734–1802)
and John Hoppner (1758–1810). Hogarth's *Miss Mary Edwards*,
signed and dated 1724, is a remarkable portrait of an even more remarkable woman. Miss Edwards, one of the wealthiest women of her
generation, was an arch non-conformist who at twenty-four inherited
an income of about £60,000 a year. She secretly married Lord Hamilton before 1731, bore him a daughter, later disowned him and denied
the marriage in order to save her fortune. Hogarth himself had run
away with the headmaster's daughter while at boarding school. This
portrait conveys Miss Edwards' shrewd disposition and unbashful
presence.

The spirit of 18th century French aristocratic life is perhaps no-
where more convincingly evoked than in the presence of Fragonard's
four large canvases displayed on the walls of the room bearing his
name and decorated with contemporary woodwork and furniture. All
the late 18th century love for mythology, classic motifs, romantic
setting, its idealization of nature and its overwhelming decorative
sense can be felt in these vivid panels. The rococo aesthetic of the
undulating line combined with stark light effects lends an almost
43 mystical dramatic tension to the events of the *Pursuit* and the *Meeting*,
two of four panels commissioned, but ultimately rejected, by Madame
du Barry in 1775 for her famous pavilion at Louveciennes.

Jean Honoré Fragonard (1732–1806) was born the son of a glove
in Grasse and later moved with his father to Paris as a young boy. He
studied first with Chardin, then with Boucher, and later became a close
friend of Hubert Robert, whose landscape style influenced him greatly.
He was eventually elected to the Académie Royale and received the
title *peintre du Roi*, but the French Revolution dealt a crushing blow to
him and his art, and he died in 1806, impoverished and forgotten.

IV   One of the greatest paintings in New York is Giovanni Bellini's *St*
Francis in the Frick Living Hall. Begun about 1479, it may be con

III. (opposite above) *The Hunt of the Unicorn. II The Unicorn at the Fountain*,
late 15th century; French or Flemish 145 × 149 in. (368·3 × 378·4 cm.)
The Metropolitan Museum of Art, The Cloisters Collection
IV. (opposite below) Giovanni Bellini, *St Francis in Ecstasy*, begun c. 1479
oil on canvas 49 × 55$\frac{7}{8}$ in. (124·4 × 141·9 cm.)

dered a culmination of nearly all important currents in quattrocento
t. It is a powerful and beautiful fusion of naturalism and super-
aturalism. Shown as a hermit, the saint stands alone in the full bloom
f his manhood, intelligent and aware before a bright glow in the
:y, which symbolizes in naturalistic terms the vision of Christ on the
ross by which St Francis received the stigmata. The humility of the
aint is emphasized by the vastness of the landscape around him; his
ove for animals is alluded to by the presence of a donkey, some birds,
nd a rabbit who pokes his head from a hole in the small stone wall.
he 15th century's enormous interest in the variety of the natural
vorld is here given expression through the combination of elements
f both the Tuscan and Flemish landscape traditions. The luminosity
f the surface is the result of colour glazes, a technique which became
haracteristic of later Venetian painting.

Titian's portrait of *Pietro Aretino* (1492–1556), the Italian dramatist
nd satirical poet (who ròse from a kitchen servant to become one
f the most feared men of his generation), is thought to have been
ainted shortly after 1548. Many of Aretino's writings were so caustic
nat in 1527 he was forced to flee the wrath of Pope Clement VII and
ake up residence in Venice, where he and Titian became close friends.
he painting shows a massive man who dominates the canvas pic-
orially and psychologically. It is one of Titian's best portraits.

Approximately contemporary with Titian was the Augsburg-born
ierman painter Hans Holbein the Younger (1497–1543) who studied
vith his famous father, then settled in England in 1532 and worked in
he society around Henry VIII, where he became friends with the great
lumanist Erasmus of Rotterdam. The portrait of *Thomas More* is
lated 1527. More, famous Humanist and theologian, was beheaded
y Henry VIII for his refusal to subscribe to the Act of Supremacy
vhich gave to the King the last word in matters of religion as well as
tate. It was in More's house that Erasmus wrote his famous satire
incomium Moriae to which Holbein made pen and ink illustrations.
he portrait of More, completely devoid of any Mannerist pretentions,
eveals the forceful temperament of one who could stand up to such
 man as Henry VIII and die for his convictions. By the same token,
he portrait of *Sir Thomas Cromwell* reveals all the qualities of con-
niving political slyness that made Cromwell largely responsible for

.3 (opposite above) Jean Honoré Fragonard, *The Pursuit*
iil on canvas 125¼ × 84⅞ in. (318·7 × 215·5 cm.)
.4. (opposite below) Claude Lorraine, *The Sermon on the Mount,* 1656–59
iil on canvas 67½ × 102¼ in. (171·4 × 259·6 cm.)

More's death and finally resulted in his own undoing by Henry i
1540.

El Greco's portrait of *St Jerome as Cardinal* dates from about 159(
and is supposed once to have hung in the cathedral of Valladoli
St Jerome is the author of the first translation of the Bible into Lati
(4th century) and one of the four Fathers of the Church. Tradition h;
made him into a Cardinal. Greco's painting is so full of individualit
and character that it was long thought to represent a contemporar
16th century personality.

John Constable (1776–1837), one of the first and greatest c
modern landscapists, painted *Salisbury Cathedral* in 1826, when h
style had just matured. Constable himself declared it the most difficu
landscape he had so far attempted. The fidelity with which the arti
rendered the details, matched with his constant attention to the ove
all design, is quite as remarkable as his intimate understanding of th
nature of things as distinct as Wiltshire cows and Gothic architectur

The most famous painting in the North Hall is the *Virgin and Chi*
with Saint Catherine and Donors by Jan van Eyck and his assistan
Petrus Christus (*c.* 1410–1473). The painting reveals all the jewe
like preciosity of Jan's work: the intricate cloth designs, the finel
painted town-scape; but the kneeling Carthusian and the nun at th
right, with their round faces and rather stubby bodies, are more aki
to the style of Christus. The painting is thought to have been don
between 1441-and 1445 for Dom Jan Vos, Prior of the Carthusia
monastery of Val-de-Grace near Bruges.

Paolo Veronese, so called after his birthplace in the North Italia
town of Verona, is the author of two large canvases in the West Ga
lery, *Wisdom and Strength* and *The Choice of Hercules*, both of whic
show the rich colour of the Venetian tradition. The feeling for move
ment in space and the interplay of light among forms, seen in both, a
important elements in the formation of Baroque painting during th
17th century. A student of Pontormo, the Florentine Bronzino (1503
1572) painted the imposing portrait of young *Lodovico Cappor*
probably between 1550 and 1555. The elongated proportions of th
body, the somewhat affected pose and the urbane self-consciou
expression of the face are characteristic of Central Italian Mannerisn
in the 16th century.

Georges de La Tour is well known for his luministic paintings lik
the Frick *Education of the Virgin,* where a single light source lend
unity to the composition, gives a volumetric appearance to the forn
and a mystical connotation to the event which is otherwise shown i

aturalistic terms.

Four paintings by the Antwerp-born Frans Hals serve to document s reputation as the first great painter of Protestant Holland. The *ortrait of a Man*, c. 1655, illustrates Hals' late style — broad, quick rush strokes and a kind of transitory animation in the face.

Of the eight paintings by Anthony van Dyck (1599–1641), only a ew are usually on view. One of the finest is the *Portrait of Frans nyders* who, along with Van Dyck, was an assistant in Rubens' shop. an Dyck's own personality was somewhat less forceful than that of is master, and he therefore achieved a greater fidelity and sensitivity capturing a personality. The perfect balance of component elements the composition is complemented by the graceful painting of the ands and the sense of quiet animation evident in the face.

Several excellent landscapes are in the same room. The earliest is by acob van Ruisdael, along with Hobbema, the leading landscapist of is generation. *Landscape with a Foot Bridge*, 1652, is a beautiful vocation of the Dutch countryside with figures in the foreground. All ne colours are pure and distinct and there is a feeling of solidity and nate goodness that seems to permeate the earth and sky.

The two large Turners facing each other on opposite sides of the oom, *The Harbour of Dieppe*, c. 1825, and *Cologne*, 1826, were xhibited at the Royal Academy in London where they were criticized or the bright, almost monotone colour which was felt to be too far emoved from nature. Turner, however, was concerned not with truth o nature, but with pictorial reality. In this, and in his understanding f the fusion of colour areas in the retina of the beholder, he is a fore-unner of the Impressionists. *The Lake* by Jean Baptiste Camille Corot aused even harsher criticism when it was exhibited at the Salon of 861. In it we see how far ideas of landscape had come since Van Ruisdael. The singularity of the whole and the integrity of perspective elationships are violated in favour of a decorative lyricism spreading colour over the surface of the canvas in the manner of an Oriental silk attern.

The *Portrait of Nicholas Ruts*, 1631, is still signed with the initials Rembrandt used while in Leyden before coming to Amsterdam. It is he earliest Rembrandt in a New York museum and, when compared vith his two later paintings in the same room, it becomes very nstructive. Rembrandt shows himself bound by tradition and youth o the careful delineation of form, each element of the composition leserving equal attention. In *The Polish Rider*, c. 1654, the linear

45. (left) Rembrandt van Ryn, *Self-portrait,* 1658
oil on canvas 52⅝ × 40⅞ in. (128·5 × 103·8 cm.)
46. (right) Diego Velasquez, *Philip IV of Spain,* 1644
oil on canvas 51⅛ × 39⅛ in. (129·8 × 99·3 cm.)

boundaries around forms begin to disintegrate. The horse is seen a
flickering highlights of white. Details of costume, upon close examina
45 tion, are mere blotches of colour. The late *Self-Portrait,* 1658, is th
epitome of Rembrandt's art. He is concerned only with essences, onl
with inner being. Every brushstroke contributes to one image, on
idea. The interplay of light and shadow has become almost violent a
the huge chest and intense face loom out from the darkness. When h
painted this portrait, Rembrandt had run the full gamut of conven
tional success and failure. He was bankrupt, living virtually at th
mercy of his creditors, yet his creative genius was at its height and hi
intense gaze seems to reflect the bitter irony of a world which has s
often forced genius to beg.

46   *Philip IV of Spain* (1605–1665) was decidedly not the *beau idea*
of kingship regarding matters of state, but his connoisseurship wa
beyond reproach. For his private summer residence, Buen Retiro, in th
suburbs of 17th century Madrid, he collected one of the finest artisti
treasures ever assembled. He also discovered and patronized one o

e greatest painters who ever lived, Diego Velasquez. The Frick
ortrait was painted in 1644 while he was with his troops at Fraga in
atalonia, attempting to put down the French-aided Catalan uprising.
was copied at once, and one of these copies was hung in the
athedral of Lérida where it was on view the day of the king's entry
to the town. The virtuosity of Velasquez' brush is particularly notice-
ole in the decoration of the king's cloak and in the fine work of the
anderlyn collar.

The Forge is one of the best Goyas in America. Painted around
318, it is remarkable for its precociousness, paying tribute neither to
e coolness of academic neo-classicism nor to romantic emotiona-
m, but achieving elements of realism not to appear in European
ainting for another thirty years.

The enamel room contains examples of painted Limoges enamel
om the end of the 15th through the 16th century. The greatest
moges enamel painters came from two different families; the
Snicaud, the greatest exponent of which was Nardon, and the
mosin who followed them. The large triptych, probably by Nardon
mself, shows the great master's style in all its colour and richness.

Duccio di Buoninsegna was the most important Sienese painter
the 13th century, a contemporary of the Florentine Cimabue. His
mptation of Christ is from the back of the great *Maestà* painting in   47
e Siena museum. It was commissioned in 1308 and finished in 1311,

47. Duccio di Buoninsegna,
The Temptation of Christ,
1308–11
tempera on wood
17 × 18¼ in. (43·1 × 46·3 cm.)

when it was carried in a long procession through the streets of t
town to the cathedral. The theme of the altarpiece itself is the glorific
tion of God. The scene in the Frick panel comes from Matthew 4:8—1
and is a fascinating combination of medieval symbolic concepts ar
incipient dramatic realism. The scale of figure to building and lan
scape does not follow the rules of scientific perspective. Christ, t
devil, and the angels are more important and so they are larger; als
the kingdoms of the world are not actual places, but symbols
luxury and indulgence, and as symbols they are governed by symbo
and not scientific perspective.

The long panel with the representation of a saint, perhaps *St Jo*
the Evangelist, is from an altarpiece by Piero della Francesca (*c.* 141
1492), painted for the church in his birthplace, Borgo San Sepolc
Piero's return to the solid monumentality of Masaccio is evidenc
here in the rock-like drapery which differs from the lyric and flowir
qualities of his contemporaries, Botticelli and Fra Filippo Lippi.

The Oval Room contains two Gainsboroughs, *Mrs Baker*, 178
and *The Honourable Frances Duncombe, c.* 1777. The latter is a ma
nificent example of the English full-length portrait and a technic
masterpiece as well, recalling Velasquez in the treatment of satin ar
lace and the great landscapists of Holland in the sky and backgroun

The paintings in the East Gallery are moved more often than tho
in other parts of the museum, but among the masterpieces which te
to remain on permanent exhibition are several of extraordinary quali

44 The large *Sermon on the Mount* by Claude Lorraine (1600—1682), t
great French landscapist who spent much of his life in Italy, w
acquired by the Frick Collection in 1961. It is the sole representati
of this subject (Matthew 5:7) by Claude. We know from his not
books that he attempted to achieve some measure of geographic
accuracy by consulting a map of the Holy Land. The view looks
from the valley of the Jordan to Mount Tabor; on the left is the De
Sea, on the right, the Sea of Galilee. The multitudes, gathered to he
the Sermon, are dispersed in small groups at the foot of the mounta
where Christ and His disciples are seated. Claude has used a ve
bright blue for the robes of a number of figures in various parts of t
painting in order to unify the composition and to offset the genera
low tonal key.

The Lady with the Serinette by Jean Baptiste Siméon Chard
(1699—1779) is probably the artist's second wife. The paintir
though done in 1751, has more in common with 17th century Dut
painting than it does with 18th century French neo-classicism. T

oft light and mellow tones recall Vermeer.

In the *Comtesse d'Haussonville* by J. A. D. Ingres, finished in 1845, we see the artist at the height of his creativity. He spent nearly four years working on the portrait, and we know from his letters that it posed several acute problems for him—not the least of which was his sitter's pregnancy in 1843. The Comtesse was herself an artist and a broadly-educated woman of excellent lineage who had published several books, among them one on Lord Byron. Ingres has captured the very essence of her intelligence and self-possessed charm. This, combined with the compact design and careful placement of objects, makes the painting one of Ingres' finest portraits.

There are few modern painters more dogmatic about their theories on art than was James Abbott McNeill Whistler, and none of his paintings better illustrates his insatiable desire to perfect his ideas than does the portrait of *Mrs Leyland* which was never really completed. Born in Lowell, Massachusetts, Whistler later became a close friend of Oscar Wilde. The incisive, at times caustic, wit of the two men had much in common. It was after an argument resulting from Whistler's having decorated a room in Leyland's home with peacocks, symbols of pompous egotism, directed at her ship-owner husband, that Mrs Leyland banished the painter. Whistler was one of the first painters to take an interest in Japanese art, and in this portrait, one of his most ambitious, the flat, light-toned surface reveals a keen feeling for pattern and design. The pigments used here were so thin that they sometimes ran on the canvas, and time has made them so transparent that one can trace the numerous and tedious reworkings that Whistler hoped would result in an impression of spontaneity.

The director of the Frick Collection is Harry D. M. Grier.

The museum is opened weekdays 10 a.m. to 6 p.m., Sundays and holidays 1 p.m. to 6 p.m. It is closed Mondays and January 1, May 30, July 4, Thanksgiving Day, and December 24 and 25. In June, July and August it is opened Wednesdays and Sundays 1 p.m. to 6 p.m., Thursdays, Fridays and Saturdays 10 a.m. to 6 p.m. and is closed Mondays and Tuesdays. From October to May there are free illustrated lectures at 3 p.m. each Wednesday. Chamber music concerts are heard in the winter on Sunday afternoons, and there are daily organ 'interludes' at 11.30 a.m., 12.30 p.m. and 4.30 p.m. Children under 10 years are not admitted, groups may visit by appointment only and no cameras are permitted. Postcards, reproductions and greeting cards are for sale in the lobby.

The Audubon Terrace

Broadway betwen 155th and 156th Streets
IRT Subway (Broadway), 157th Street Station;
Fifth Avenue Buses 4, 5

**including the Hispanic Society of America
the Museum of the American Indian
the American Numismatic Society
the American Geographical Society**

48 The Audubon Terrace is a complex of buildings grouped round a central court on Broadway between 155th and 156th Streets. The land once belonged to the American artist John James Audubon (1785?–1851) and was purchased by Archer Milton Huntington for the establishment of a cultural centre for specialized study. The institutions presently housed there are: the American Academy of Arts and Letters, the National Institute of Arts and Letters, the American Geographical Society, the American Numismatic Society, the Hispanic Society of America and the Museum of the American Indian. Each is a privately supported, non-profit organization.

The **American Academy and the National Institute** hold exhibitions of art and literature containing the work of newly elected members and award winners. The exhibitions change frequently and the institutions should be contacted for specific information. They are open daily 2 p.m.–5 p.m. during exhibitions, closed on Mondays and holidays.

The **American Geographical Society** owns the largest private geographical library and map collection in the Western Hemisphere; it is open to the public Monday to Friday 9 a.m.–4.45 p.m.

The **American Numismatic Society** has the only museum in the world devoted entirely to numismatics. There are two modern exhibition halls, one devoted to the development of coins from their beginnings some 2,600 years ago until today; the other is devoted to medals and decorations of honour, where the displays trace the development of medallic art from its origin in the Renaissance to modern times. It is open Tuesday to Saturday, 10 a.m.–5 p.m. and closed Sundays, Mondays and holidays.

48. The Audubon Terrace

The **Museum of the American Indian** was opened in 1922. It was founded by Dr George C. Heye in 1916 for the purpose of furthering knowledge concerning the Indians of all the Americas. Developing from the private collection of Dr Heye, it is now the largest Indian museum in the world. The institution is concerned with both the prehistoric development of man in the Western Hemisphere and the contemporary Indian. The exhibits feature many examples demonstrating the aesthetic achievements of the pre-Columbian Indian in North, Central, and South America. They are arranged on three floors, by tribe and area.

On the first floor the exhibits are concerned with the tribes of the eastern and mid-western United States. An entire display case is given over to Iroquois masks used in rituals often originating in prehistoric times and still in practice today. They represent mythological beings who have the power to dispel evil influences and to cure the sick. The masks of the Iroquois were not assembled, but carved from one piece of wood, then painted with earth and vegetable pigments.

The way of life of the Indians of the Great Plains was the most recent to develop and the one to receive the most publicity through cinema, television and popular literature. It is certainly one of the most colourful of all. After the introduction of the horse by the Spaniards, many of the sedentary tribes became nomadic and joined together in pursuit of the buffalo, which provided them with food, shelter, clothing, and weapons. This culture was born, flourished and died in the brief period of two hundred years. The objects that the Plains Indian created were small and portable, the ideas of movement and speed everywhere being evident. The use of fringe, so common to western U.S. clothing, was an attempt to imitate the feathers of birds and to give the effect of increased speed.

One of the most interesting examples of the art of the Plains Indians is a painting of a *Horse Raid* done about 1875 with vegetable pigments on smoked buffalo hide. Only the men of the tribe were allowed the freedom of representative art; the women worked in abstract designs.

The Seminole were from the southeast and excelled in appliqué work. A man's costume shows the technique at its best. The enormous dexterity in workmanship and the sophistication in design are evidence of a mature tradition.

Also from the southeast, rare beadwork, pottery and basketry illustrate the depth and range of the Indian culture whose present shameful state of decay will remain always a black stain on the pages of western history.

The second floor of the museum, perhaps the most interesting, will be open to the public in the near future after extensive remodelling. The displays will be given over to the archaeology of North America. A prehistoric mask carved from a solid piece of wood comes from the Spiro Mound in Oklahoma. A bowl in the shape of a wood-duck carved from a solid piece of diorite comes from Moundville, Alabama and dates between 1200 and 1600 A.D. It is perhaps the finest example of Indian craftsmanship in North America, and can certainly be compared for design and quality of workmanship with contemporary examples from Europe and the East.

Some of the most interesting and popular art comes from the north west coast of America, the strip of land including eastern Oregon, Washington, Canada, British Columbia and Alaska. The abundance of forest land gave rise to magnificent sculpture in wood. A mask representing *The Octopus Man* comes from Bella Bella, British Columbia and is inlaid with haliotis shell and painted with large bright red lips. A large Raven Mask (about a yard in length) comes from Vancouver Island and is part of the ritual paraphernalia of the Hamats Society. The great beak opens and closes on a leather hinge as the wearer moves his head up and down. The designs are carved in low relief and painted in with red, yellow and white to form a most impressive expression of Kwakiutl art.

From the trunks of the giant trees of the northwest, the Indians of that region created some of the most monumental wood sculpture to be found anywhere. One cannot help but be awed by the dominating presence of the huge sculptured jamb figures twelve to fifteen feet in height and a yard in diameter representing guardians and anthropomorphic spirits. From the same area come giant ceremonial feast dishes the size of bathtubs, carved in animal shapes from tree trunks

49. (left) Seneca masks from the Cayuga and Onondaga Grand River Reservation, Ontario, Canada. The Museum of the American Indian
50. (right) Luis Morales, *Virgin and Child with a Distaff* oil on panel 28½ × 19⅛ in. (72·5 × 48·5 cm.) The Hispanic Society of America

The singular skill with which the craftsman worked is easily seen in the regularity of the adze marks in the wood which show no evidence of having been re-worked.

Baskets were an essential part of Indian life and on the second floor is a large variety of shapes and sizes from many different tribes.

The Hopi Indians of the southwest are responsible for some of the finest pottery of the Americas. They are sedentary and live in 'pueblos' or small villages. The Kachina dolls of the Hopi are small wood carvings representing the costumed dancers who take part in the pueblo ceremonies. They are used as teaching devices for children, so that they may learn to understand the rituals. The Zuñi and Navajo of New Mexico still produce beautiful silverwork often decorated with turquoise stones and mother of pearl.

The third floor is devoted to the art and archaeology of Central and South America and the West Indies. From Colima in western Mexico there are numerous redware figurines and vessels which date from the 4th to the 10th centuries A.D. From the same period in Oaxaca in

Central Mexico come the elaborately decorated funerary urns made of clay in shapes representing Zapotec deities. The earliest artefacts yet excavated from the Western Hemisphere, up to 1000 years B.C., are very attractive bowls, bottles and flasks. There is a large display of Aztec and Mayan stone sculpture and rare wood masks and shields inlaid with turquoise mosaic from the Mixtec culture. Throughout Middle America archaeologists have found tiny clay figurines, sometimes painted, in a variety of postures. Their exact function is not known and they are here displayed as though partaking in everyday village life. Carved alabaster vases and polychrome pottery from the Ulúa Valley of Honduras, cylindrical polychrome jars decorated with painted friezes from El Salvador and Nicaragua, figure sculpture in jade and green-stone, carved mace heads from Costa Rica and the beautiful and richly painted ceramic plates and vessels from Panama give a well-rounded view of the artistic creation of the Central American peoples up to the time of the Conquest.

From the West Indies Islands come examples of stone sculpture and pottery. The oval shaped stone rings are thought to be belts worn by the natives during games.

From South America there is outstanding Colombian gold work, painted Inca keros shaped like animal heads from Peru, and from the southern Peruvian Nazca culture comes much of the best designed and decorated pottery in all South America, some in the shape of small rodents sitting upright and holding their bellies with both hands. There are also richly decorated and exquisitely made fabrics from ancient Peru as well as exhibits of the arts of Ecuador, Brazil, Venezuela, Guatemala and Guyana.

The director is Dr Frederick Dockstader.

Books on Indians, Indian handicrafts, toys and souvenirs are for sale in the lobby. There is no guide service. The hours are 1 p.m.–5 p.m. Tuesday to Sunday; closed Mondays and holidays.

The **Hispanic Society of America** was founded in 1904 by the great American hispanophile and man of letters, Archer Milton Huntington (1870–1955). The society was created to house the private collection of books, manuscripts, and works of art that Mr Huntington had collected – mostly from places outside Spain, since it was his policy not to remove works of art from their country of origin. The library and museum comprise one of the most important centres for research on the culture of the Iberian peninsula in the United States. The collection includes paintings, sculpture, ceramics, metalwork, furniture, textiles, maps, and books, largely from Spain, but also from Portugal and South America. The sales desk, located in the Sorolla Room, has some of the most reasonably priced postcards and books to be found in the city. For fifty cents one can take a tape-recorded tour of the museum.

Most impressive of all the Hispanic Society's collection, and perhaps best representative of the Spanish genius itself, are the paintings. In the middle of the 15th century, more than a hundred years after Giotto had painted the Arena Chapel in Padua, and several decades after Masaccio had laid the foundations for a Renaissance style of painting — when the art of Jan van Eyck was in full bloom in Flanders, much Spanish painting still remained under the spell of early medieval traditions. It harboured a conservative, largely two-dimensional, intensely religious art that borrowed some ideas and techniques from Flanders and Siena, but gave in only very slowly to the spatially orientated and more secular art of Florence.

On the left of the main-floor entrance is a panel showing *St Vincent* with a palm leaf, symbol of his martyrdom. Against a richly tooled gold background, he stands triumphant over an exotically turbaned Moor who writhes at his feet. St Vincent becomes analagous with good and the Moor (like the dragon he resembles) is evil defeated. Most of the panels along this wall once formed parts of large pictorial and sculptural complexes called 'retablos' which were often located in one of the many chapels of a cathedral or behind the main altar of a smaller church. The Catalan panel showing the *Virgin and Child Enthroned* once must also have formed part of a 'retablo.' The raised gold halos are characteristic of the Spanish and particularly the Catalan craftsman's preoccupation with decorative surface.

Other notable paintings of the 15th century include five panels from a Castilian 'retablo,' an *Enthroned Virgin and Child* by Pedro Romano, a tiny *Nativity* panel from the Valencian school, and the Aragonese 'retablo' of the *Visitation*. The latter is interesting not only for its comparative lack of foreign stylistic influences, but also for its strange and graphic portrayal of the *Visitation*, where an image of the Child appears as a small infant suspended between Mary and Elizabeth radiating points of shimmering light.

From El Greco's early Toledan period the Society has a *Pietà* and a *Holy Family*, which show clearly the artist's Venetian training and his use of certain Mannerist devices. These, however, he uses not in an attempt to achieve elegance, but to spiritualize and enhance the deeply religious subject of the painting. Mystical elements are further brought out in the *St Jerome* portrayed as an old hermit with a long white beard who stares with transfixed gaze upon the image of the Saviour on the Cross. The *Supper in the House of Simon* attributed to Jorge Manuel, El Greco's son, reveals a new interest in still-life which was to become of major importance in 17th century painting.

A generation younger than El Greco and a native Spaniard from Badajoz in Extramedura was Luis Morales, called El Divino (the divine) (*c.* 1520–1586). The Society's *Virgin and Child with a Distaf* shows the deep sense of mood and mystical presence in his characters that won him an unshakeable place in the popular mind of the Spanish people. In the *Ecce Homo* he invests the mocked Christ with a profound pathos, while creating in the expression of the eyes and lips a mere adumbration of the confidence born of Christian humility. *The Holy Family* is most important for its grand conception, combining several figures in a deep landscape with a horoscope of Christ in the upper righthand corner.

Antonio Moro (Anthonis Mor) (*c.* 1519–*c.* 1576) was born in Utrecht, Holland. He worked at the court of Charles V of Spain and the Netherlands, the court of Portugal, England, and for Philip II of Spain. Moro is very important in the formation of Spanish painting and for state portraiture generally. It was his stiff and formal portrait style which was emulated by others, and which remained for generations the official style of the Court portrait. An excellent example is the supposed portrait of the *Duke of Alba*, (*c.* 1549). The hieratic and still manner tended to raise the sitter to an ideal plane and make him personification of his own rank and office.

The two paintings by José de Ribera (1591–1652) are among the finest in the collection. The full-blown Baroque qualities of light and volume can be seen in the *Ecstasy of St Mary Magdalen* as she rises amongst billowing drapery and a throng of chubby angels. The *St Paul* shows an assimilation of the techniques of the Italian *tenebrosi*. In its massive form, serious and straight forward depiction of the king who converted to become a disciple and a saint, Ribera illustrates the Counter Reformation's firm rejection of the frivolous and vulgar in its art.

The greatest painter of monastic life in 17th century Spain, Francisco de Zurburán, excelled also in the depiction of solitary female saints, shown dressed in rich gowns of silk and carrying the symbol of their martyrdom in their hands. The Hispanic Society's *Santa Rufina*, perhaps the best of the three Zurburáns on exhibit, becomes a pretext for the painter to put on canvas the grace and elegance of Sevillian women. Just as the male saint was hero, the female saint became heroine, possessed of all the qualities of high birth, dignity

1. (left) Diego Velasquez, *Portrait of a Little Girl* oil on canvas
$)\frac{1}{4} \times 16\frac{1}{8}$ in. (51·5 × 41 cm.) The Hispanic Society of America
2. (right) Anonymous, *Mater Dolorosa,* 13th century polychromed wood
 ∍ight $50\frac{3}{4}$ in. (129 cm.) The Hispanic Society of America

 ιtelligence, and religious devotion.
   Velasquez moved from Seville to Madrid in 1623 and his greatest
 ιme derives from his portraits of the court of Philip IV. He found favour
 οt only with the king, but with his minister, Gaspar de Guzman,
 ʹount-Duke of Olivares, whose large, full-length portrait in the
 ιispanic Society he painted during his second trip to Madrid. The
 ʹiff and formal style contrasts markedly with the Society's other three
 οrtraits, *Cardinal Camillo Pamfili,* a *Portrait of a Moor,* and a *Little* 51
 ʹirl. This last is certainly one of the finest portraits in New York.
   This was the great age of Spanish painting, its *'Siglo de Oro'.*
 ∍esides names like Velasquez, Zurburán, Ribalta, Ribera, Murillo,
 .ere were others, only less renowned by comparison with the great
 ιasters. The Hispanic Society has on display paintings by Collantes,
 ιonso Cano, Valdés Leal, Escalante, and Carreño de Miranda.
 ʹarreño's large *Immaculate Conception* on the second floor balcony,
 ʹgned and dated 1670, is a magnificent work which reveals the

artist's predilection for delicate colours and deep, encircling baroque space. The curiously bizarre painting on the opposite side of the balcony by Sebastian Muñoz was ordered by the Shod Carmelites of Madrid. It shows Maria Luisa of Orléans, wife of Charles II and Queen of Spain (d. 1689), on her great death-bed dressed as a nun, surrounded by attendants, candles, cherubs, incense smoke and a priest.

In sharp contrast to the 17th, the 18th century seemed to hold no promise of greatness for Spanish painting until in 1746, in the little Aragonese village of Fuendetodos, a genius was born. Francisco de Goya y Lucientes stood entirely alone as an artistic force in the midst of economic, social and moral decline. His style changed from the elegant, playful tapestry designs to the biting satire of *Los Caprichos* and the symbolic horrors of the *Black Paintings*. Like his English contemporary, the satirist Jonathan Swift, Goya was a rationalist who spent his life in constant battle against ignorance and superstition.

53   The Hispanic Society has four Goyas. The large *Duchess of Alba* is dated 1797, shortly after the Duke's death. The much discussed relationship between her and Goya, and whether the *Nude Maja* in the Prado is really Alba painted from life, is made even more enigmatic by the curious attitude of the Duchess and by the two rings she wears. One is inscribed 'ALBA,' and the other, 'GOYA'. The index finger of her right hand points to the ground where the words 'SOLO GOYA'– Goya alone!–and the date are written in longhand. The word 'SOLO' uncovered in cleaning, may have been painted over at the Duchess' request. Perhaps she was unwilling to go quite so far with the painter' indecorous joke. She is dressed 'à la maja,' in the popular style of the 18th century Spanish aristocracy who affected the flamboyant costumes of the lower classes, much as fashion in the later 1960's has turned for inspiration to the gangster world of the 1930's.

The three-quarter length portrait of *Pedro Mocarte* on the second floor balcony is also one of the best Goyas in America. Mocarte was a choir singer in Toledo Cathedral and seems to have been a close friend of the painter. He is dressed in the splendid suit of a torero, his hair tied back in a bun, his rough but kindly face contrasting somewhat with his elaborate shirt and cape. The painting of *Albert Foraster* signed and dated 1804 unfortunately has undergone many changes and extensive restoration. In the exhibit room at the top of the stair the individual leaves of Goya's *Los Caprichos* are displayed. These

53. (opposite) Francisco de Goya, *The Duchess of Alba*, 1797
oil on canvas $82\frac{7}{8} \times 58\frac{7}{8}$ in. (210·2 × 149·3 cm.) The Hispanic Society of America

idactic etchings with subtitles are an important key to much of the
rtist's later work.

A great friend of Archer M. Huntington, the society's founder, was
oaquin Sorolla y Bastida (1863–1933). A native of Valencia who
emained there all his life except for trips of short duration, Sorolla
egan as a painter of history, anecdotes and intimate scenes recalling
ne art of Bastien Lepage. His style began to change in the mid-1890's
nd he found the perfect unity of colour and subject matter in his native
alencia. One cannot fail to respond to the magnificent series of
nurals in the Sorolla room representing *The Provinces of Spain*. The V
ffects of brilliant light, the irresistable variety of textures, the flashing
olour of costume, of skin and hair and water, and the sense of move-
nent and immediacy make this room one of the most exciting in the
ity.

Among the earliest objects from the museum's collection of pre-
istoric and later works of art are two black earthenware bowls of the
ate Neolithic–early Bronze age, which were found at Los Alcores
ear Seville in Andalucia. The culture that produced them probably
xisted about 2500–2000 B.C.

The Iberian peninsula was rich in natural metals, especially copper,
on and silver. The Society has a variety of Bronze Age implements
hat show the progressive advances made in technology and func-
ional design.

From the Iron Age there are expertly made bronze bracelets, fibulae
sed in place of buttons and zippers, belt buckles, and bronze
tatuettes, such as the small winged boar from the Island of Menorca
ff the Valencian coast, *c.* 500 B.C.

The Romans invaded the Iberian peninsula in 218 B.C. and though
he Celtiberians put up a fierce battle, the great Imperial machine
inally had its way. By about 100 B.C. a flourishing Roman civilization
vas established which lasted until the beginning of the 5th century
..D. From Italica, the first Roman settlement in Spain, the Society has
2nd century A.D. marble bust of a *Young Man* and a Roman copy of
Greek marble *Artemis*. There are also examples of Roman floor
nosaic, now displayed on the walls of the stairwell. On the second floor
alcony are many pieces of Hispano-Roman jewellery and pottery.

. (opposite above) Joaquin Sorolla y Bastida, *Ayamonte – Men Hauling Tunnies
rom the Wharf* from the series *The Provinces of Spain*, 1911–19
il on canvas 137$\frac{3}{8}$ × 191 in. (349 × 485 cm.)
I. (opposite below) Vincent van Gogh, *Starry Night*, 1889
il on canvas 29 × 36$\frac{1}{4}$ in. (73·5 × 92 cm.)

On the opposite side of the balcony is a larger case showing one of the finest collections of Hispano-Moresque lustreware in America. The pieces are notably of the 15th and 16th centuries. The bright metallic colours and dynamic patterned designs are the work of expertly skilled craftsmen, who, because of the demands of the medium, had to work even more quickly than the frescoist.

In the stairwell, along with the pieces of Roman mosaic, are scores of examples of Hispano-Moresque and later tile and tile mosaic. At the top of the stairs are a number of examples of Moorish grave slabs with Arabic inscriptions, and a 10th century Hispano-Moresque marble basin.

The intermingling of the Islamic and Christian traditions is visible in much art produced in Spain during the Middle Ages, as can be seen in the large collection of ironware on the second floor balcony which includes door knockers, nail heads, keys, fragments from *rejas*, and other pieces ranging in date from the 14th to the 18th century.

The Society's collection is also rich in gold and silver work, most of which is to be seen in the large display cases on the first floor. There are examples of processional crosses, croziers, monstrances, patens and other liturgical items through the 18th century. Most interesting is a 17th century silver incense burner from Argentina in the shape of a fan-tailed turkey. Also in the same case are Spanish ivory carvings.

52 One of the Society's most important pieces of sculpture is the 13th century polychromed wooden *Mater Dolorosa* with hands clasped to her breast. The two massive marble tombs of Gutierre de la Cueva and Mencia Enriquez de Toledo of the 16th century mark the transition from Gothic to Renaissance. Of the several 16th and 17th century marble effigies of aristocratic personnages, two are by the Italian Pompeo Leoni. Perhaps most characteristically Spanish in style is the 17th century *Mater Dolorosa* elaborately polychromed and gilded with flying baroque drapery and dynamic contraposto.

Outside the building are two huge reliefs by Anna Hyatt Huntington, wife of the founder, whose sculptured animals grace several locations in the City. On the left is Boabdil, the last of the Moorish kings of Cordoba; on the right, the defeated Don Quixote. Appropriately placed between the two is her large equestrian bronze statue of El Cid Campeador.

The director is Theodore S. Beardsley, Jr.

The museum is open Tuesday to Saturday 10 a.m. to 4.30 p.m. and Sundays from 2 p.m. to 5 p.m. It is closed on Mondays and on major holidays.

The Museum of Modern Art

11 West 53rd Street
IND Subway (E or F train), Fifth Avenue Station

The Museum of Modern Art was founded in 1929 by five pioneer 54
American collectors—Miss Lillie P. Bliss, Mrs John D. Rockefeller, Jr,
Mrs Cornelius J. Sullivan, A. Conger Goodyear and Frank Crownin-
shield, its stated purpose being 'to help people enjoy, understand, and
use the visual arts of our time.' Since then the museum has mounted
numerous loan exhibitions, sponsored travelling shows to many parts
of the world and has played a major role in the dissemination of ideas
and the formation of high standards of taste. With its various depart-
ments—photography, industrial design, prints and drawings, painting
and sculpture—and through its numerous special exhibitions, publications and lectures, the museum reaches a wide public and is one of
the City's most important and most heavily attended cultural institutions. The building was designed by Philip Goodwin and Edward
Durell Stone and was opened in 1939.

The present collection, the most important of its kind in the world,
contains about 20,000 works of art, of which nearly 2,000 are paint-

54. (left) The Museum of Modern Art
55. (right) The Abby Aldrich Rockefeller Sculpture Garden

99

56. Henri Rosseau,
The Dream, 1910
oil on canvas
80½ × 117½ in. (206·4 × 298·3 cm

ings. The galleries are arranged and numbered chronologically, th
works of a particular school, artist or style usually being found togethe

The work of untutored artists, often called primitive or naïve, is t
a large extent timeless, ignoring historical styles and changes in tast
Naïve paintings of all periods share many things in common: a genera
disregard for scientific perspective, a tendency to fill all existing spac
with line or colour, and a wide popular appeal.

One of the greatest masterpieces of naïve painting in modern time
54 is Henri Rousseau's *The Dream*, 1910. Rousseau (1844–1910), calle
Le Douanier because he made his living as a minor customs offici
on the outskirts of Paris, was born in Laval, France. *The Dream* revea
a remarkably sophisticated sense of colour and design, a bold an
fertile imagination unfettered by artistic convention. Every leaf
placed with exacting precision, each form is carefully modelled.
quiet geometry pervades the entire painting; the woman's breasts a
drawn with a compass, her toes and fingers have no joints. There a
no blemishes or imperfections anywhere, and everything exudes
mysterious, primeval sensuousness, the rhythm of which seem
dictated by a tune from the native green piper emerging from th
foliage. Rosseau explained the painting this way: 'This woman aslee
on the couch dreams that she has been transported into the fore
listening to the sounds of the enchanter's instrument. This is the reaso
the couch is in the picture.'

The style of Joseph Pickett's masterpiece, *Manchester Valle*
1914–1918, derives from the old tradition of American sign painte
and limners. Pickett (1848–1918) was a canal-boat builder, a carpent
and later a store keeper. During the summer he sometimes operated

ooting gallery at a county fair. He painted landscapes like *Man-
ester Valley* as backdrops for his galleries. Distance is rendered not
rough scientific perspective, but by placing nearer objects at the
ottom and distant ones at the top. The enormous quantity of detail
ay be equated with a desire for exact documentation, the painting
f things 'just as they are in real life.'

Claude Monet carried the tenets of Impressionism farther than any
f his contemporaries, working in the style when others had long
nce abandoned it. *Water Lilies,* 1920, consists of three large panels
overing three walls on the second floor with shimmering light and
ater. The finest examples outside the Orangerie in Paris, they were
quired to replace the Monets destroyed in a museum fire in 1958.
hey are important as an example of the synthesis of abstraction with
aturalism and are an anticipation of later currents.

Cézanne's *Bather, c.* 1885–1890, is one of his most monumental
aintings of the single human figure. Flattened out like a cement slab
gainst an ill-fitting landscape background, the figure (probably
rawn from a photograph of the model) takes on a profound sense of
ability and permanence. The rendering of anatomical parts (the right
rm, right knee and foot) are not correct, but the effect of the whole is
ne of poise and bearing.

It was Vincent van Gogh, however, a mystic, a profound moralist,
athologically concerned for the collective soul of mankind, who
ansformed the objective Impressionist eye into a subjective,
ynamically charged vision. *The Starry Night* is an imaginative inven- VI
on, a topography of the mind and not of the world, for surely no
rovençal town ever had a Northern Gothic church like the one in the
icture. No stars ever hung like great yellow egg yolks while a violent
ky of blue swirls all about them and the Milky Way twists itself in a
not.

The first of the 20th century artistic revolutions arose in France in
e years 1898–1908 with a group who exhibited in the famous
alon d'Automne of 1905, forming themselves around Matisse who
as the innovator and recognized leader of the movement. *Les Fauves*
as the group was called), a term coined by the same critic who coined
ubism, means 'the wild beasts' and was thought effectively to
escribe those who made a barbarous use of colour, often spreading
directly from the tube, no mixing, no brush! A somewhat subdued
xample is *Blackfriars Bridge, London,* 1906, by André Derain
1880–1954), where the departure from naturalistic colour exceeds
ll previous movements of the 19th century. The Thames is composed

57. (left) Henri Matisse, *The Red Studio*, 1911
oil on canvas $71\frac{1}{4} \times 86\frac{1}{4}$ in. $(80 \cdot 9 \times 219$ cm.)
58. (right) Max Beckmann, *Departure* (left hand panel of triptych), 1932–35
oil on canvas $84\frac{3}{4} \times 39\frac{1}{4}$ in. $(214 \cdot 9 \times 99 \cdot 6$ cm.)

of bright dashes of yellow, blue and green. A tug-boat is a smear o
blue with a dash of white at bow and stern for its wash. Suc
'haphazard' and unceremonious use of colour was heresy in Paris a
the turn of the century.

57   By 1911, when he painted *The Red Studio*, Matisse (1869–1954
was no longer under the spell of the Fauves. In this large canvas, h
plays a daring and subtle game with colour and the elements of com
position. The red ground tends to flatten the picture into a near ab
straction. The paintings placed about the studio relate to one anothe
colouristically, but it is the understated use of thin white lines for th
borders of furniture and floor which gives the slight illusion of space
The eye is made to see both pattern and depth all at once. Th
museum also has Matisse's *The Dance*, 1909, the first large sketc
for one of his most famous paintings.

Georges Rouault (1871–1958) also exhibited with the Fauves a
the *Salon d'Automne* in 1905. *Three Judges*, 1913, shows him to b
closer to the German Expressionists in mood however. A friend of th
neo-Catholic convert Huysmans and the Catholic philosophe

Jacques Maritain, Rouault was deeply involved in a kind of neo-medieval Thomism which he expressed in his paintings, themselves somewhat medieval in feeling. Judges are one of his favourite themes. He shows them here culpable, utterly mortal. The huge figure in the centre is more stupid than evil, a complete reversal of the quasi-divinity of the great judges of Christian history. The sombre colours reinforce the mood; the black outlines are traceable to Rouault's work in stained glass.

Of the same generation as Matisse and Rouault in France were the German Expressionists Barlach, Nolde, Kokoschka, and Beckmann. One of the most impassioned, Oskar Kokoschka (b. 1886) grew up in the Vienna of Freud and Mahler (whose widow he was to marry) to become Austria's greatest painter. *The Portrait of Dr and Mrs Tietze,* 1909, the great scholars of Venetian painting, is rendered in thinly superimposed layers of colour in order to capture the vibrant quality of life in the hands and faces.

The three large panels of *Departure,* 1932–1935, by Max Beck- 58 mann (1884–1950) recall nothing so much as a late medieval scene of martyrdom as represented by German and Spanish artists. Painted at a time when many refugees were fleeing the horrors of Nazi Germany, Beckmann among them, the painting seems a poignant comment on world affairs at the time.

Modigliani (1884–1920) left a life of poverty in Italy in 1906 to join the international 'School of Paris' along with Picasso, Braque, Delaunay, and Brancusi whose simplified sculptures were an inspiration to him. *Reclining Nude, c.* 1919 (Modigliani called it his *Gran* 59 *Vu*), is one of his best paintings. The torso is slightly elongated and stylized by placing an area of dark beneath the waist and by exaggerating the curve of the hips. Entirely lacking in prurience (not easily said of many earlier French and Italian nudes), the figure attains a true

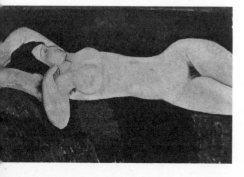

59. Amedeo Modigliani,
Reclining Nude, c. 1919
oil on canvas
$28\frac{1}{2} \times 45\frac{7}{8}$ in. (72·3 × 116·5 cm.)

60. Pablo Picasso,
Les Demoiselles d' Avignon, 1907
oil on canvas
96×92 in. (243·8×233·6 cm.)
61. (opposite) Pablo Picasso,
Guernica, 1937
oil on canvas
138×308 in. (350×782·3 cm.)

dignity and monumentality through its formal balance. The museum
also owns *Bride and Groom*, 1915–1916, and *Anna de Zborowska*
1911, wife of the Polish poet Leopold Zborowska who aided
Modigliani financially and helped him gain recognition.

The greatest figure of the School of Paris, and the most important
painter of the 20th century, is Pablo Picasso (b. 1881). For his
earlier, pre-Cubist work we must look to the Guggenheim Museum
and to the Metropolitan Museum of Art, but the Museum of Modern
60 Art owns what has justly been called the first Cubist painting, *Les
Demoiselles d'Avignon*, 1907, one of the great monuments of 20th
century painting. Picasso made many preliminary sketches before he
attempted the full-scale painting. It is looked on now as a battleground
where a young genius is attempting to create a new expression from
his own visual experience of archaic and primitive sculpture, fashion-
ed by his traditional understanding of form and colour. The result,
though not entirely successful as a work of art, was to have a profound
influence on the 'cubist generation' of Paris. Picasso's search for
meaning and expression beyond the tenets of naturalism and realism
led him to investigate the aesthetic geometry of pre-Christian Iberian
sculptures (the figure at extreme left) and West African Negro masks
(face at upper right). The title, humorously donated by a friend of
Picasso, refers to Avignon Street in Barcelona and to the prostitutes
who worked there. *Girl Before a Mirror*, 1932, is a veritable text book
on the art of design. Colour and line and the 'positive-negative' play
on shapes reflected in a mirror reveal psychological implications as
well. The girl may be holding a mirror, but what she sees reflected in
it is a Cubist X-ray *à la Freud*.

Picasso is a great artist not merely because he knows where to put

what colour or because he has the 'audacity' to innovate. His genius
is informed by a deep and compassionate concern for human beings,
by a broad and searching intellect that despises complacency, which
is why he was able to say that for him painting was not made to
decorate apartments, that it was a weapon of attack and defence
against the enemy. It's not what the artist did that mattered, but what
he was. Cézanne teaches us of restless striving and Van Gogh of
emotional torment. Picasso's most famous painting, *Guernica*, 1937, 61
was commissioned by the Spanish democratic government for the
Spanish pavilion at the Paris World Fair. It has been on loan from the
artist to the museum since 1939. While he was planning the composition, the news reached Picasso that on April 26, 1937, the tiny Basque
village of Guernica had been the target of the first air attack in history
on a civilian population. It was on a market day; the people and
animals were crowded in the streets and squares. They looked up
quizzically at the sound of planes. Within a matter of minutes Guernica
was a burning heap of humans and animals, of Romanesque churches
and Gothic houses. Hitler's German Condor Legion, under the orders
of Generalissimo Franco, systematically and effectively destroyed the
town. Picasso's painting of the event is not narrative. It does not
'describe' the systematic bombing of Guernica; rather, it is imagistic
and expressive. It is a pictorial metaphor for pain, agony, destruction.
Heads, exploded hands, hoofs, dislocated arms, severed breasts, loose
eyes, all mingle amidst the screams of men, women and animals. All
superfluous elements of design are left out; the colours are black and
white and grey. The painting deals only in essences, with the immediate horror made eternal.

Night Fishing at Antibes, 1939, is an unusual Picasso and one of his most brilliant achievements in colour harmony. The painting, nc without a sense of humour, shows a weary, grey fisherman spearing very picassoid sole while another fisherman leans over the side t stare disjointedly at a paper-thin fish and a cross-eyed urchin. This perhaps Picasso's most important painting of the decade followin

61 *Guernica.* The rather gay mood may reflect a feeling of optimism i the few months after the end of the Spanish Civil War and before th start of World War II.

Many of the elements of Surrealism are anticipated by Mai Chagall (b. 1887). In *I and the Village,* 1911, the artist constructs pictorial image of his own past in his native Vitebsk, Russia. It is healthy and a happy image of a life where man and beast see eye t eye, where girls milk cows and men work in the fields. The Cros appears twice; once on the church steeple and once around the nec of the smiling man. The scene derives its effectiveness from conder sation, both of time and place. Like the brief few seconds at the end c a dream, there is a summing up and a fusing of sights and feeling

62   Paul Klee's *Twittering Machine,* 1922, is a brilliant drawing (watei colour, pen and ink) that partakes of several modes of expression a once: the visual, the literary, and the musical. In his diary, Klee ha written that he never illustrated a literary motif, that he has made plast form, and only afterwards taken pleasure when a poetic and a plasti idea 'accidentally' coincided. Such is the case here. A perfect unity implied musical harmony from the alto of the figure on the left to th base of the figure next to him is combined with the formal rhythm of th wonderfully expressive spring-like figures whose movement is cor trolled by the crank of the machine which we are told is 'twittering

Giorgio de'Chirico (b. 1888), an important forerunner of th Surrealist movement, was intent on restoring to painting a poet mood in spite of a contemporary anti-Romantic reaction. His *Nostalg. of the Infinite,* 1913–1914, creates a feeling of overpowering lone liness and distance by its implied diminution of the spectator (throug exaggerated perspective) and utter lack of movement except for th fluttering of flags on the top of the red roofed-tower.

With Salvador Dali (b. 1904) Surrealism is in full bloom. *The Pei sistence of Memory,* 1931, is his most famous painting and perhap his best. The effect of disquieting mood is achieved through an illusio of vast distance, by the violation of the laws of physical proportior of familiar objects, by the creation of quasi-real forms and throug juxtaposition of different textures having certain sensorial connota tions.

2. (left) Paul Klee, *Twittering Machine,* 1922
watercolour, pen and ink $16\frac{1}{4} \times 12$ in. (41·2 × 30·4 cm.)
3. (right) Edward Hopper, *House by the Railroad,* 1925
oil on canvas 24 × 29 in. (60·9 × 73·6 cm.)

Other Surrealistic or fantastic paintings include Peter Blume's *The Eternal City,* 1934–1937, where fantasy is combined with precise naturalism to produce a somewhat bathetic allegorical indictment of Mussolini's fascist Italy, Paul Klee's *Around the Fish,* 1926, Miró's *Dutch Interior,* 1928, and Pavel Tchelitchew's *Hide and Seek,* 1940–1942. The latter depicts a phantasmagoria of children's heads and limbs among intertwined capillary systems growing from a tree, while a heavy-legged girl wanders deeper into the maze.

A sudden flowering of art in Mexico was the result of a long tradition of primitive styles enhanced by the discovery of modern Western art and kindled by revolutionary ideas about freedom. The movement was begun by Diego Rivera (1886–1957) and continued by Orozco (1883–1949), Siqueiros (b. 1898), and Tamayo (b. 1899). Rivera's large *Agrarian Leader Zapata,* 1931, in fresco, shows the style in all its earthy monumentality. Emiliano Zapata, greatest name in modern Mexican history, commanded an army of farm-labourers during the 1910–1920 revolution. He is shown again along with his famous guerillas in huge sombreros, with bayonets and cross-belts of ammunition in Orozco's *Zapatistas,* 1931. The rhythm of the forms repeated in the red and white colours creates a massive forward moving force. Siqueiros' *Echo of a Scream,* 1937, is a fantastic image of

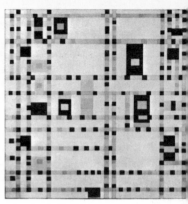

64. (left) Andrew Wyeth, *Christina's World,* 1948
tempera on gesso panel 32¼ × 47¾ in. (81·9 × 121·2 cm.)
65. (right) Piet Mondrian, *Broadway Boogie Woogie,* 1942–43
oil on canvas 50 × 50 in. (127 × 127 cm.)

industrial waste and poverty. An excellent work by Rufino Tamayo is
Animals, 1941, where the daring combination of bright red with blue
and green adds to the ferocity of the strange dogs.

In American painting after the World War I there was an in
creasing tendency to abolish investigations of formal problems in
favour of a return to nature. A new realism arose and looked to aspects
of American life for its subject matter. The leading painter of this pro

63 vincial American scene was Edward Hopper (1882–1967). His *House
by the Railroad,* 1925, was the first painting to enter the museum's
collection. The lack of any vegetation or sign of human or animal life
gives the large Victorian house a desolate, lonely appearance, aug
mented by the colour blue and by the cast shadows beneath the
Mansard roof.

64   Andrew Wyeth's *Christina's World,* 1948, is rendered with the pre
cision of a Bellini, but the worm's eye view and the exaggerated
perspective give the scene a surrealistic feeling.

Ben Shahn (b. 1898) has been an articulate voice in defence of a
'humanistic' art of representation. But his *Handball,* 1939, reveals
however, a fascination with large colour areas treated as pure form.

Jack Levine (b. 1915) refers to himself as a 'romantic humanitar
ian'. His criticism of the evils of man in society are well seen in *The
Feast of Pure Reason,* 1937, done for the Federal Art Project of the
Works Progress Administration. Levine has compared the artist to a
magistrate who must sit in judgment and make an intelligent evalua

ion of any aspect of humanity he chooses to deal with, the validity of his art being dependent upon the humanity of his decision.

John Marin (1870–1953) has drawn from a variety of European Modernist tendencies of the first half of the 20th century. *Lower Manhattan*, 1920, is one of his most famous watercolours. Not as abstract as it might first appear, one recognizes in it the towers of the Woolworth building above the Third Avenue Elevated. Marin was excited by the dynamic transition from a Victorian New York to a New York of skyscrapers and elevated highways, and this excitement is plainly revealed through the vigorous movement of the lines and colours of his composition.

Piet Mondrian (1872–1944), a Dutchman and one of the pioneers of Abstract art, left Cubism for pure geometric abstraction. *Broadway* 65 *Boogie Woogie*, 1943, his last completed painting, is inspired by the dynamic rhythms of American jazz. The use of primary colours carefully placed in varying sized rectangles creates a sensation of movement akin to that of the persistent base rhythm with accompanied flights of melody which characterizes the music of the same name.

After the close of World War II, both Europe and America saw the rise of Abstract Expressionism. It was during these years that Tobey, De Kooning and Pollock made New York as important a world art centre as was Paris during the rise of Cubism. Jackson Pollock (1912–1956) developed a technique known as 'action painting' where he placed an unstretched canvas on the floor and dribbled and splashed paint from a can, moving all around the canvas, stooping, bending and leaning. In this way Pollock felt 'in' the painting. He compared his method to that of the Indian sand painters of the West. Such was the way he painted *Number I*, 1948. His interest is not in subject mat- 66 ter but in expression through the *act* of painting itself.

De Kooning's expressionism is somewhat less abstract. *Woman I*, 1952, is a most controversial painting and one which has won great favour among contemporary young artists. The seemingly haphazard application of paint is in fact the result of intense concentration and great knowledge about colour and its effects. The glaring seated female is so alive with violent hostility, so devoid of conventional platitudes about femininity that it seems a painted attack on 'The Fabulous Fifties' of Hollywood movies and men's magazines.

It was inevitable that a reaction to the deeply subjective nature of Abstract Expressionism should occur, and thus the movements known as Op and Pop use a highly disciplined, precisionist technique controlled by an objective point of view.

66. (left) Jackson Pollock, *Number 1,* 1948
oil on canvas 68 × 104 in. (172·7 × 264·1 cm.)
67. right) Vern Blosum, *Time Expired,* 1962
oil on canvas 37½ × 27⅞ in. (95·2 × 70·7 cm.)

Ad Reinhardt (b. 1913) in his *Abstract Painting,* 1960–1961, has coloured nine separate squares with shades of brown-black so close in proximity to each other that a sign next to the painting tells the visitor to look closely or he will mistake the nine areas for one. Such carefully premeditated visual effects are the complete opposite of expressionism.

Pop art, meaning simply 'popular' in reference to the subject matter is one of the newest movements to date. The technique is usually hard edge painting, drawing inspiration from popular, commercial and advertising art. *Time Expired,* 1962, by Vern Blosum (b. 1936) is a carefully painted picture of a parking meter. All the lettering is completely readable; it is true to nature in the strictest sense of the phrase. It is a kind of contemporary American still-life, an acceptance of the parking meter as a common sight in an urban environment, and an affirmation of its validity, along with telephones and Coke machines, as a subject to be painted.

Sculpture is distributed throughout the museum galleries and in a special area on the third floor. The Abby Aldrich Rockefeller Sculpture Garden on the ground floor contains Lachaise's *Standing Woman,* Rodin's *St John* and Matisse's *Four Reliefs of Backs,* among others.

Maillol's *Seated Woman, c.* 1901, later named 'The Mediterranean' to suggest the timeless calm and serenity of the figure, recalls pre-classic Greek sculpture and the clearly defined volumes of Cézanne

Wilhelm Lembruck (1887–1919) combined the classic poise of Maillol with a Gothic elongation to achieve poetic and expressive figures like his *Standing Youth*, 1913, and *Kneeling Woman*, 1911, two of the finest of 20th century sculptures.

Cubist sculpture is rare, and *The Horse*, 1914, by Raymond Duchamp-Villon (1876–1916) is perhaps the greatest example. Boccioni (1882–1916), as a leading Futurist, was interested in motion and speed. His *Unique Forms of Continuity in Space*, 1913, is the product of many drawings and models of the human figure in violent motion. One of the most important sculptures of modern Italy, it attempts to represent the impress of moving forms upon the atmosphere itself.

Constantin Brancusi (1876–1957) made a return to primary forms, essences and archetypes, taking his inspiration from West and Central African sculpture. *Bird in Space*, 1919, is not an abstraction of a bird, but an image of flight itself; *Fish*, 1930, one of his most significant works, reaches beyond all description and imitation to arrive at an archetypal form embodying the subtle curves and sure balance of a great fish in water.

Alberto Giacometti (b. 1901) has constructed the equivalent of a surrealist painting in his *The Palace at 4 p.m.*, 1932–1933. This wood-glass-wire-string cage records surrealistic metaphors from the artist's own experiences with a woman in whose company, over a period of six months, he made a number of match box houses. He is more familiar today for his needle-like human figures of rough cast bronze, the *Chariot*, 1950. Perhaps also inspired by Surrealism, Julio Gonzalez (1872–1942), a Catalan like Picasso whom he taught to work in iron, established wrought iron as an important medium for modern sculpture. His *Head, c.* 1935, has been an important influence on sculptors, the crescent-shape becoming almost a sculptural cliché in the 1950's.

On the first floor there are two small alcoves and a display cabinet devoted to the sculpture and jewellery of the American Alexander Calder (b. 1898). His huge mobile *Lobster Trap and Fish Tail*, 1939, actually exists in four dimensions. The slightest breeze will set the intricately balanced forms in motion. Such sculpture in its responsiveness to its environment is like a leaf that moves in the breeze, or a fish moved by the currents of the water.

Behind a plexiglass shield on the third floor is the intricately designed *Variation Number 7: Full Moon*, 1944–1950, by Richard Lippold (b. 1915). The ten foot web is made of brass rods, nickel-chromium and stainless steel wire. Lippold has said that patience and

68

68. Richard Lippold,
Variation Number 7:
Full Moon, 1949–50
brass rods,
nickel-chromium and
stainless steel wire
height 120 in.
(304·8 cm.)

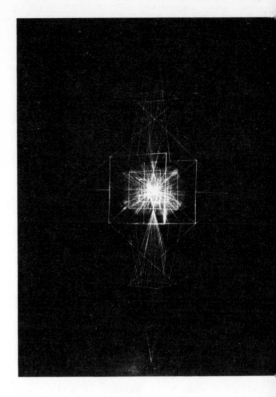

love gave life to the work, and that patience and love must be em
ployed in all dealings with it; its hanging and its seeing.

It is on the third floor also that one finds the Edward Steiche
Photography Center where an excellent collection of photographs b
such greats as Stieglitz, Man Ray and Dorothea Lange is on changir
exhibit. Next door is the gallery of prints and drawings with an exce
lent showing of American prints. A large sales counter near th
entrance to the museum carries a variety of books, pamphlets, mag
zines and reproductions. A garden restaurant on the ground flo
serves complete luncheons, teas and dinners on Thursdays only. The
is a penthouse restaurant for members. Special events include dai
film showings at 2 p.m. and 5.30 p.m., Thursdays at 8 p.m. and Satu
days at 11.30 a.m., 3 p.m. and 5.30 p.m. There are art classes for
ages as well as a picture lending service, concerts and lectures.

The director is Bates Lowry.

The museum is open daily 11 a.m. to 6 p.m., Thursdays 11 a.m.
9 p.m. and Sundays 12 p.m. to 6 p.m. It is closed Christmas Day.

The Jewish Museum

09 Fifth Avenue at 92nd Street
T Subway (Lexington) 96th Street Station; Fifth
enue Buses 2, 3, 4

ne Jewish Museum, under the auspices of the Jewish Theological
eminary, displays the largest collection of Jewish ceremonial objects
existence. Four floors of the old Felix Warburg mansion have been
ven over to the display of both the permanent collection of older
eremonial art, and modern works made by the Tobe Pascher Work-
op of Contemporary Jewish Ceremonial Objects, which is housed
the basement of the museum and is a division of the Seminary's
chool of fine arts. The museum was begun in 1947 when Mrs
Varburg donated the mansion on 92nd Street, a landmark of the
ench Renaissance style in New York. In 1962 it was enlarged by
vice its original size through the gift of the Albert A. List Building
ext door, designed by Samuel Glaser.

On the second floor, one of the greatest treasures of the museum is
ne gold Torah crown from Poland studded with jewels and dated in
ne second half of the 18th century. It is placed on the rolled Torah it-
elf in recognition of the sacred nature of the text. Torah headpieces,
hich are smaller individual crowns, are placed on the ends of the
nafts and removed before the service. Since it is forbidden to touch
ne sacred text, gold or silver Torah pointers are used to follow the
ords, the reading of which forms the central part of Jewish ritual.
here are several Torah arks in the museum, large wooden cabinets
hich frame and hold the scroll when not in use. The breastplate
hich hangs over the rolled Torah has been the cause for much
plendid decoration in gold and silver in accordance with the words
om Exodus: 'This is my God and I will glorify Him.'

In medieval times spices were valued so highly that they were
cked in towers for safekeeping, and thus a tower-like shape became
aditional for spice containers used in the home during the celebration
f Passover. The museum's collection, beginning roughly in the 15th
entury, comes from many parts of the world.

The festival of Hanukkah celebrates the re-dedication of the Temple
Jerusalem after the victory of Judas Maccabaeus over the Syrians.
he eight lights of the Hanukkah lamp symbolize the eight days during

69. The Jewish Museum

which the miraculous cruse of oil (which was quantity enough for on
day only) burned in the Temple. During the festival itself, a light
ignited the first night, two on the second night and one on each suc
ceeding night until all eight are lit. Because of the sanctity of the lam
with eight flames, it could not be used for practical purposes and so
ninth was added in succeeding ages (called the *Shammas* or servai
light) in order to utilize the lamps for needed lighting. The exhib
illustrates a development from the simple clay oil lamp of Roman time
to more complex types developed later. The Hanukkah lamp eventua
ly took the shape of the seven-flame Menorah, since the origin
bench type could not be efficiently enlarged to meet lighting require
ments as, in the course of centuries, Hanukkah became celebrated i
the synagogue and had to accommodate large numbers of peopl
Two lights were added to make the nine required for the Hanukka

Marriage rings in the collection were used as symbols of the legalit
of the marriage contract and were often the property of the congrega
tion, to be worn by the bride for a week after the ceremony and the
returned.

Other objects of special interest are the impressively decorated 18
century silver Torah Cases, the Torah Shrine of faïence mosaic fror
northeast Persia, *c.* 1500, the well displayed collection of Hebre

). Second floor of the museum showing Jewish Ceremonial Art

ɔins, and a collection of bronze portrait plaques of famous Jewish
ᴉen.

Much can be gained from a study of the traditional forms of Jewish
ᴇremonial art in comparison with the modern objects made by the
ʳaftsmen who work in the basement of the museum. These modern
ᴇremonial pieces show both an attempt to keep tradition alive within
ᴉe context of contemporary design and a healthy attitude that seeks
ɔnstantly to examine, interpret and beautify the symbols of faith.

One of the most important and renowned functions of the museum
; its sponsorship of changing exhibitions of contemporary art. Past
ᴉows have included the work of Max Ernst, Philip Gaston, Larry
ivers, Jasper Johns, Robert Rauschenberg and Ad Reinhardt. A
ᴉotographic exhibition entitled *The Lower East Side: Portal to
merican Life,* 1966, was so popular that it was repeated. One should
ɑll the museum to find out what exhibition is presently being held.

The director is Sam Hunter.

The hours are Mondays through Thursdays 12 p.m. to 5 p.m.,
ʳidays 11 a.m. to 3 p.m., Sundays 11 a.m. to 6 p.m., closed Saturdays.
ᴉere is a sales desk in the lobby which has information on exhibitions
nd publications pertaining to the collection. Guided tours are avail-
ɔle upon advance application.

The Solomon R. Guggenheim Museum

1071 Fifth Avenue at 89th Street
IRT Subway (Lexington), 86th Street Station; Fifth
Avenue Buses 2, 3, 4

71 Solomon R. Guggenheim (1861–1949), industrialist, philanthropis
and patron of art began collecting paintings before World War I. A
first he favoured largely Old Masters, American landscapes and work
of the French Barbizon school. Then in the late 1920's, he began t
collect 20th century painting, especially the more advanced examples
He had the Solomon R. Guggenheim Foundation incorporated i
1937, and in 1939 a temporary museum was set up at 24 East 24t
Street. In 1943 Mr Guggenheim commissioned Frank Lloyd Wright t
design a museum for his collection. Before his death in 1949, he ap
proved Wright's plan, and by 1951 the Foundation had purchased th
entire block on 5th Avenue between 88th and 89th Streets. The build
ing was opened to the public on October 21, 1959.

Frank Lloyd Wright, who studied with Louis Sullivan in the 1880's
is recognized as the founder of a uniquely American architecture. Th
Guggenheim Museum, which poses revolutionary ideas about urba
architecture and museum display, was his last great achievement an
his only one in New York City. The purpose behind the design of th
building is to achieve a new unity between the beholder, the paintin
and the architecture. Wright claimed it was not to be a 'cellular com
position of compartments, but one where all is one great space on
continuous floor. The net result of such construction is greater repos
an atmosphere of the unbroken wave – no meeting of the eye wit
angular or abrupt changes of form.' He conceived the building a
'woven' rather than constructed and more like sculpture than archi
tecture. Its chief virtues would be lightness and strength.

The building contains 7,000 cubic feet of poured concrete and 70
tons of structural steel. The six-story structure is cylindrical with
hollow centre. One takes the elevator to the upper ramp and descend
at a gentle 3 per cent grade to the lobby. Illumination is achieved b
72 means of natural light entering through the wire-glass dome, and wit
artificial light both reflected and intensified by use of a continuou
mirror (invisible to spectators), and adjustable plastic blinds.

The permanent collection of paintings and sculpture is vast. It con

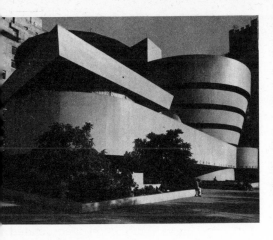

1. (left) The Solomon R. Guggenheim Museum
2. (right) Interior view

ains the largest single collection of the works of Chagall, Delaunay,
ileizes, Léger and Franz Marc in the United States. There are over 180
andinskys and over 170 Klees, and a very good representation of
eurat, Cézanne, Rousseau, Derain, Bonnard, Picasso, Braque,
Modigliani, Miró, and Mondrian. Recently there has been a strong
mphasis on sculpture, especially Brancusi.

Like most museums, the Guggenheim's permanent collection is far
n excess of existing exhibition space and therefore only a small por-
on of the paintings and sculpture can be seen at any given time. The
nly exhibition area where paintings are not changed from time to
me is the third floor galleries given over to the newly acquired Justin
. Thannhauser bequest (opened April of 1965). The largest and one
f the finest of the paintings in these galleries is *The Hermitage at* 73
ontoise, c. 1867, by one of the oldest of the Impressionists, Camille
issarro (1850–1903). Born in the Virgin Islands, the son of a Portu-
uese Jewish father and a Creole mother, Pissarro later went to Paris
nd became a leading Impressionist and a major influence on
Cézanne. At Pontoise (north of Paris) he painted several versions of
he Hermitage, this version being one of the least impressionistic and
nost serene and intimate.

Renoir (1841–1919) painted the large *Woman With a Parrot* about
871. The model is Lise Tréhot (1848–1922), a postmaster's daughter
vho lived with Renoir from 1866 to 1872, and posed for many of the
rtist's paintings during those years. In this early work one is aware of

close affinities with Manet (cf. his *Woman With a Parrot* about 186(in the Metropolitan Museum of Art); an emphasis on rich colour and subdued light. It is one of Renoir's last works before he began to pain the dazzling light-filled pieces of his Impressionist period.

The several Cézannes in the Thannhauser galleries include a *Portrait of the Artist's Wife, c.* 1886, and two fine still-lifes from the latter 1870's showing the solid colours and rhythmic geometry with which Cézanne built up his compositions. Quite the opposite is Van Gogh's *Mountains at Saint Rémy,* 1889, where all is writhing move ment and turbulence. The paint is laid on thickly and decisively. The technique of painting wet on wet lets the top coat pick up the colou beneath, adding resilience, depth and complexity to the colours.

Of the numerous Picassos on view, several are worthy of specia attention. The *Moulin de la Galette,* 1900, is the first work the young Picasso executed in Paris. One immediately thinks of the famou: Renoir version of the same subject in the Louvre, painted just twenty one years earlier. But Picasso is here closer to Toulouse-Lautrec than to Renoir. The Impressionist *joie de vivre* has become almost carica ture. A sinister, self-conscious leer appears on many faces. Detail is kept to a minimum and the figures are subjected to an overall patterr that tends to de-emphasize their humanity. *Woman Ironing,* 1904 is from Picasso's Blue Period, 1901–1906, during which time the young artist concentrated on a kind of Gothic stylization of figure: with great metaphysical depth. The use of blue creates a sense o mystery which is reinforced by the elongated body of the woman *Three Bathers,* 1920, brings the discipline of the harmony of human proportions to bear on line and colour. The effect is complete balance quiet and simplicity. The marvellous face of *Françoise Gilot,* 1947 shows Picasso's brilliant decorative sense in the use of simple line.

Other works in the Thannhauser galleries include several fine Picasso drawings, Degas pastels, Rouault's *Christ and the Fishermen c.* 1930, and two large panels by Vuillard of the *Place Vintimille* in Paris. Cézanne's *Man with Folded Arms, c.* 1895–1900, by its solid and classical pose recalls the artist's own statement that he wished to make of Impressionism something lasting 'like the art of the museums.

The Guggenheim has two of several excellent paintings in New York by Henri Rousseau (Le Douanier) (1844–1910). *Artillerymen, c* 1895, possesses all of the stiff, self-conscious charm of an early photograph. Part of the naïve quality comes from the frankly com memorative mood of the scene. *A Game of Football,* 1908, depend: for its intensely pictorial quality on the suspended animation of the

73. Camille Pissarro, *The Hermitage at Pontoise, c.* 1867
oil on canvas $59\frac{1}{2} \times 78\frac{3}{4}$ in. (151·1 × 200 cm.)

players and on the 'unreal' field bordered by strictly symmetrical rows
of trees. This is a purely aesthetic world where every natural form is
deftly placed and controlled by the artist. Accident, so important to
Baroque and Impressionist painting, is completely absent here.

Three fine Modiglianis reveal the artist's interest in African sculpture, in the works of the old masters and in his contemporaries,
especially Cézanne and Picasso. His superb understanding of line and
pattern is evident in *Yellow Sweater,* 1919, where the entire right out-
line of the figure is one gently undulating curve from the head to the
floor. The *Nude* of 1917 and the *Boy in a Blue Jacket* of 1918 are two
more outstanding Modiglianis in the collection.

Marc Chagall (b. 1889) is represented by several works, the most
famous among which being *The Soldier Drinks,* 1912–1913, and *Paris* IX
Through the Window, 1913. The soldier, like the fiddler, the milkmaid
and the street sweeper, are characters from the artist's youth in a tiny
Russian village. He once called his pictures 'painted arrangements of
inner images that obsess me.' *The Soldier Drinks* uses the formal idiom
of Cubism to express the images stored in the artist's mind. The paint-

74. Robert Delaunay,
St. Severin, 1909 oil on canvas
$44\frac{7}{8} \times 35\frac{1}{8}$ in. (97·4 × 89·2 cm.)

ing is not surrealistic, but realistic and narrative, the imagery being
representational rather than abstract or symbolic. The close-kni
world of the soldier is summed up in the uniform, the small wooder
house, the bar, the glass and the two tiny dancers who frolic like
marionettes before his eyes.

Robert Delaunay (1885–1941) came to Cubism by way o
Cézanne's Post-Impressionism. He very quickly outgrew the narrowe
analytic Cubism and interested himself in the rhythms of architecture
74 and cities. He painted *St Severin* in 1909. Fascinated by the forms o
Gothic architecture, he attempts to render the over-all rhythm and
dynamism of the piers and vaults. About a year later, in 1910, his style
underwent a change and he became more interested in form. He began to paint various versions of the *Eiffel Tower* (1904, 1910, 1912)
The integrity of the object itself is lost in a pile of clouds, buildings
trees. He painted *Circular Forms* about 1912 or 1913. Now interested
solely in colour, he felt that art must free itself from the object, otherwise it remains merely descriptive, doomed to servitude and imitation

Wassily Kandinsky (1866–1944) left his work in the field of political
economy and law at the age of thirty to devote his time to art and
aesthetic theory. Along with Franz Marc, he founded the Blue Rider
Group of German Expressionists who sought the spiritual and mystical
75 from form and colour. The large *Study for Composition No. 2,* 1909,
shows a festive scene; a wooded landscape with hills, two leaping
horses and riders facing each other at the centre, some children playing and a couple reclining at the right. White roses and standing
figures are at the left, below, a reclining figure, and at the top a hill

5. Vasily Kandinsky,
mposition No. 2, 1910
on canvas
3⅜×51¾ in. (97·4×131·4 cm.)

with domed churches, a mountain pool with trees, and curious clouds.
The painting may be understood as a symphony where the harmonics
re based on colour rather than on musical notes. Kandinsky's work
ecame progressively more abstract until in 1913 he produced *Light
icture, No. 188* and *Black Lines, No. 187* where there is almost no
eference to natural shapes and all is expressive linear movement.
utumn and *Winter,* both of 1914, are part of a four-painting series
one for a Park Avenue apartment. They are important as early
xamples of Expressionism's change from representation to pure ab-
traction. In the mid-1920's Kandinsky began to move away from the
urging colour masses of his earlier works and to subject his colours
o a sharply defined flat geometry of circles, squares, and triangles, as
Extended, 1926, and *Two Sides Red, No. 437,* 1928, where colour
nd scale predominate in an atmosphere of calm. A synthesis of the
wo styles is reached in *Dominant Curve, No. 631,* 1936, where the
ynamic colour areas are stabilized and unified with a variety of geo-
metrical shapes and the musical feeling is intensified and sustained.
   Franz Marc (1880–1916) was concerned with the inner lives and
eelings of animals. Under the influence of a kind of modern-day
ranciscanism or neo-pantheism, he sought to interpret a world in-
abited by sleepy cows and frisky horses. *Bos Orbis Mundi,* 1913, 76
ses some of the devices of Cubism in order to depict the inner being
f the cow. The 'soul' of the thoughtful animal is seen not in her head,
ut appropriately grazing in her own stomach. *Stables,* 1913–1914,
ecomes a tight frieze of refracting mirror-like images, each form
ocked within a rigid Cubist geometry.

76. Franz Marc, *Bos Orbis Mundi,* 1913
oil on canvas 27⅞ × 55⅝ in. (70·7 × 141·2 cm.)

As mentioned earlier, the Guggenheim is a huge repository of tʰ
works of Paul Klee. As a painter who was also a musician, Klee con
posed with pictorial elements in the way that a musician works wiᵗ
notes, motifs, themes, and modulations. He was also a poet and tʰ
77 titles of his works reveal a highly imaginative use of language. *Danᴄ
Monster, to My Soft Song!* 1922, is a case in point. The poetic aⁿ
musical associations are strong as the 'monster' dances on undeⁱ
stated legs to the tune of a stick-lady who cranks a tumbledown ca
liope. The curious *Revolution of the Viaducts,* 1937, is done in cha
coal on a patterned cloth. The bare simplicity of the design and tecʰ
nique shows Klee, like Picasso, to be an artist of great resourcefulnes
Severing the Snake of 1938 again achieves its effect through concisᵉ
statement and simple design. Here, as in the *Viaducts,* texture is im
portant. The writhing forms of the snake are 'negative' areas of burla
left uncovered by the brownish-green paint and later tinted wiᵗ
colour.

Two paintings by Georges Braque (1882–1963), *Violin and Palet*
and *Piano and Lute* both of 1910, are among the best of the artist
Analytical Cubist works.

78   *The Great Parade,* 1954, was one of the last works to issue from tʰ
hand of Fernand Léger (1881–1955). It is the result of numeroᵘ
sketches and studies on the theme of acrobats, musicians, and circ

7. (left) Paul Klee, *Dance, Monster, to My Soft Song!,* 1922 oil transfer drawing with watercolour on gesso-primed canvas $14\frac{1}{4} \times 11\frac{1}{2}$ in. (36·1 × 29·2 cm.)
8. (right) Fernand Léger, *The Great Parade,* 1954
il on canvas $117\frac{3}{4} \times 157\frac{1}{2}$ in. (299 × 399·9 cm.)

eople. Léger attempted, through his simplified shapes and volumes, o express a confidence in the Machine Age and the appropriateness f 'mechanical' shapes in painting. By the inclusion of acrobats alancing within the painting and by the over-all balance of forms nd colour, Léger evokes a kind of visual pun on the idea of balance tself.

Joan Miró (b. 1893), like Picasso and Dali, is a Catalan. His ieroglyphs and pictorial symbols are inspired by the art of primitive eoples; American Indians, Eskimos, and children, and not least by nineral and sealife forms of the Mediterranean. The huge *Painting,* 953, on canvas marks a revolution in Miró's style. He had never be- ore attempted a work of such large dimensions without preliminary ketches. The paint is boldly applied *alla prima* and the forms acquire dynamic quality and an unresolved potentiality that fascinates the ye.

With the ceramicist Joseph Llorens Artigas, Miró did several large eramic murals in the 1950's. The one in the Guggenheim, entitled *licia* in memory of Mrs Harry F. Guggenheim, was completed in 79 967. The generally subdued colours with a predominance of black nd grey and the animated insect-like shapes in contorted postures onjure up a predatory world of fear and anxiety. The large ceramic rch called *Portico,* 1965, uses small pebbles from Mediterranean 72

beaches embedded in the bricks before firing. The effect is that o
a lunar, encrusted surface.

The Guggenheim's collection of the works of younger contempor
ary artists, especially those born in the 20th century, is secon
only to the Museum of Modern Art. There are usually paintings o
display by Jean Dubuffet (b. 1901). The three panels of his *Nun*
Stans, 1965, hang on the ground floor, and *Door with Couch-Grass*
1957, a kind of collage-assemblage of canvas and oil paint is usuall
on display also. Another assemblage-painting is Robert Rauschen
berg's *Red Painting* of 1953, made of a patchwork of paper, cloth and
paint. Works by Jan Muller (1922–1958), Francis Bacon (b. 1910)
Franz Kline (1910–1962), Adolph Gottlieb (b. 1903), and Jackso
Pollock (1912–1956) are also on display.

A changing selection of sculpture is to be seen on the main floor
A great mobile by Alexander Calder (b. 1898) hangs above th
fountain. The static balance of steel plates, like giant lily pads, repre
sents a real marriage between engineering and sculpture. Severa
72 pieces by Constantin Brancusi are usually on display. His *Miracl*
(White Seal) recalls some of his own statements: 'inner proportion i
the ultimate truth inherent in all things . . . beauty is absolute balance.
The several wooden figures (*Adam and Eve*, 1921) recall Oceanic ar
and the fetish symbols of primitive tribes, which were such an im
portant influence on the development of the Cubist aesthetic.

Books, postcards and information are available on the main floor
The director is Thomas M. Messer.

The museum is open Tuesdays through Saturdays 10 a.m. to 6 p.m.
Thursdays 10 a.m. to 9 p:m., Sundays and all holidays, 12 p.m. to
p.m. It is closed Mondays (except on holidays), July 4, and Christmas

79. Joan Miró and
Joseph Llorens Artigas,
Alicia, 1967
ceramic mural 97 × 228 in.
(246·3 × 579·1 cm.)

Gallery of Modern Art

including the Huntington Hartford Collection

Columbus Circle
IRT Subway (Broadway) 59th Street Station; IND
Subway (Sixth and Eighth Avenue lines) Columbus Circle Station;
BMT Subway, 57th Street Station

The Gallery of Modern Art including the Huntington Hartford Col- 80
lection, like the Frick Collection, the Guggenheim Museum and the
Morgan Library, is the work of a single man. George Huntington
Hartford, Jr, heir to the Atlantic and Pacific Tea Company fortune
(A & P food chain), has carried on a vigorous battle against 'abstract
art.' He published a book condemning it and built his own museum
to prove that 'there is a valid alternative to the dominant mode of
abstraction as an expression of the deepest currents of modern
thought and feeling.' The collection also attempts to give attention to
artists and movements currently out of vogue and to show un-
characteristic works of acknowledged masters.

The building was designed by Edward Durell Stone, who designed
the U.S. Pavilion at the 1958 Brussels World Fair and also co-designed
the Museum of Modern Art in the 1930's. It has been described as
Byzantine in inspiration, a tall white cube whose smooth surface is
relieved by colonnades at the top and perforated with border decoration on all sides.

The ground floor houses a sales desk where one can purchase
postcards, photographs and catalogues; in the basement is an
auditorium equipped for showing films. The sixth and seventh floors
contain office and storage space and the eighth and ninth are devoted
to restaurants. That leaves four floors for works of art, frequent loan
exhibitions and paintings from the Huntington Hartford Collection.
The paintings discussed here are all from the Hartford Collection, but,
with the exception of the two Dalis—*The Discovery of America by* 84
Christopher Columbus and *The Battle of Tetuán*—they are not on
permanent display. One should consult the gallery in advance to find
out when the permanent collection, which alternates with special
exhibitions, will be on view.

Dedicated as it is to less popular movements in art, the Gallery of
Modern Art is one of the few places in the City where one can see Pre-
Raphaelite paintings. In 1848, Dante Gabriel Rossetti, William Holman
Hunt and John Everett Millais founded the Pre-Raphaelite Brother-

hood in England which later took John Ruskin as its spokesman. Mid Victorian romantics that they were, the painters sought inspiration in the 'pure' and 'primitive' paintings of the early Italian Renaissance. Their paintings are characterized by noble subject matter, truthfulness to nature and extraordinary attention to detail.

Sir John Everett Millais (1829–1896) was one of the most competent of Victorian painters. He became enormously successful as an academic painter and his allegiance to the Pre-Raphaelites slowly weakened. He painted *The Huguenot* in 1851–1852, one year after the exhibition of his famous *Christ in the House of His Parents*, and two years before he was elected to the Royal Academy. *The Huguenot*, in the concentrated attention to detail and in the intricate depiction of the leaves, bricks and costume, exemplifies the Pre-Raphaelite rejection of Delacroix' quick and open technique in favour of a calculated linearism and a point of view that approaches antiquarianism. Although superficially the painting may achieve a certain outward reference to the fifteenth century, it is thoroughly romantic and Victorian in mood.

Another follower of the Pre-Raphaelites was the Englishman Sir Edward Coley Burne-Jones (1833–1898). Like his friend William Morris, he rejected joining the Church in order to paint; under the influence of Rossetti both became Pre-Raphaelites. The eight paintings of the *Perseus series*, 1884–1888, in the Gallery of Modern Art evoke a dreamy, romantic, literary never-never land of Botticelli draperies and Mantegna landscapes. The series, commissioned by the Prime Minister Arthur James Balfour, is based on William Morris' poem 'The Doom of Acrisius,' which is a re-telling of the myth of Perseus. *The Rock of Doom* and *The Doom Fulfilled* are concerned with Perseus' finding Andromeda chained to a rock after he had slain the Medusa with the help of the reflecting shield given him by Athena. In order to free Andromeda, with whom he fell hopelessly in love at first sight, Perseus had to fight and kill the monster who guarded her. In the most imaginative of the series, *The Doom Fulfilled*, we witness Perseus entangled in the monster's serpentine coils while the hero glares threatenly and triumphantly at the fiendish head he is about to lop off. The object of his heroic passion displays her sensuous back and legs while her severed chain lies limply on a slab of rock.

Contemporary with the Pre-Raphaelites was the Frenchman Gustave Moreau (1826–1898) who, in the midst of the French Impressionist movement was painting elaborate Biblical and mythological fantasies in an infinitely detailed, encrusted technique. *Salome*

0. The Gallery of
Modern Art including
the Huntington
Hartford Collection

ancing Before Herod, 1876, attempts to evoke a mysterious, in-
ense-filled atmosphere of the ancient East. The lotus flower, symbol
f voluptuousness, and the jewelled interior, rich to the point of re-
ulsion, are metaphors for the corruption of Herod's rule.

Puvis de Chavannes (1824–1898) was something of a reactionary,
ttempting to recreate the monumentality of the great Italian Renais-
ance fresco cycles. His most famous decoration is to be found in the
anthéon in Paris, for which the Gallery of Modern Art's *Childhood
f St Geneviève,* 1879, is a study in oil. The legend below the central
art of the three-piece composition tells us that in 429 A.D. St
ermain of Auxerre and St Louis of Troyes, on their way to England
fight heresy, arrived in Nanterre. Among the welcoming crowd, St
ermain noticed a child in whose face he perceived divinity. He pre-
icted to the child's parents that she would have a 'high destiny.' St
eneviève saved Paris from Attila the Hun in 451 and later she con-
erted Clovis, first of the Merovingian kings of France, to Christianity.

After the Storm, c. 1852, is a work by Paul Gustave Doré (1832–
883), one of the outstanding illustrators of the 19th century, whose
ighly original drawings for woodcuts as illustrations to the works of
abelais and Balzac are well known, though he sought in vain during

his lifetime for recognition as a painter. *After the Storm* is a character istic romantic landscape of mood with the ruins of a tower in the back ground and a rider on a white horse galloping off in the distance.

Claude Monet's *The Jetty at Le Havre,* 1868, shows the artist' early style before he painted his highly impressionistic and atmos pheric scenes like *Impression, Sunrise.* Unlike his later paintings, her the forms of the people and the lighthouse are silhouetted against th sky, treated as individual shapes, and not melted into a shimmerin haze.

Of the many fine landscapes in the Gallery, Corot's *La Solitud* 1866, George Inness' *Italian Landscape,* 1874, and Thomas Moran' *Mountain of the Holy Cross, Colorado,* 1875, are especially notabl Moran was a follower of Thomas Cole and the Hudson River painter and he combined their tradition of idealized landscape with a passio for grandeur and dramatic effect.

Reginald Marsh (1898–1954), one of modern America's mo prolific painters, has sometimes been accused of stooping to mean ingless superficiality. Such a view is itself superficial. Marsh was dedicated and meticulous seeker after the perfection of his art. Thoug born in Paris, he became the great recorder of New York City in th 1930's. Paintings such as *Wonderland Circus Sideshow, Cone Island,* 1930, and *Pip and Flip, Twins from Peru,* 1932, are characte istic of his concern, like Hogarth and Goya, for the sordid, debauche world of less enlightened areas of society. Of his subjects in the 1930 he said: 'I . . . . paid frequent visits to the beach at Coney Island whe a million near naked bodies could be seen at once, a phenomenon un paralleled in history . . . . '

Walt Kuhn (1877–1949) painted *Hand Balancer* in 1942. Most his pictures are inspired by the circus, but he rejects the cheap an showy glitter for the more personal side of performers themselves. Th intent yet unposed and unpretentious mood of the work recalls th dignity and seriousness of such great portraitists as Titian an Rembrandt.

Two huge paintings by Salvador Dali, whose name seems unavoic ably connected with the Gallery, are on permanent display in a sma room built especially for them. Dali was born in Figueras in Spanis Catalonia in 1904. He became a leading Surrealist until he disengage himself from the movement and its implied socialist doctrines to re

VII. (opposite) Stuart Davis, *Owh! in San Pão,* 1951 oil on canvas $52\frac{1}{4} \times 41\frac{3}{4}$ in. (132·7×106 cm.) The Whitney Museum of American Art

ırn to the Roman Catholic Church. His paintings reveal a deep in-
erest in the history of Spain, its art and its peculiar form of Catholic-
m. There are constant references to Catalonia and the small coastal
illages where he grew up and to local saints and historic personalities.

The Discovery of America by Christopher Columbus, 1959, is one 84
f Dali's largest paintings. According to Dr Ulloa of Figueras,
:hristopher Columbus' real name was Cristofol Colom. He was a
atalan Jew, a visionary who came under the influence of Raymond
lul, a Catalan alchemist. Colom, being a Jew, was unable to present
imself to the Catholic Monarch under his true identity, so he called
imself Cristobal Colon of Genoa. The painting emphasizes the in-
ensely religious nature of the Spanish conquest of the New World.
:olumbus is shown in the foreground about to hop onto the shore.
\t the left is the liturgical ambassador who (according to Dr Ulloa)
vas to receive Columbus in the New World: St Narcissus, patron
aint of Gerona (Catalonia) and of flies. On the right and into the dis-
ance, nude youths carry the banners of the provinces of Spain. At the
eft, the huge banner shows the Immaculate Conception, one of many
netaphors for Spanish Catholicism and the great history of Spanish
)ainting. In the foreground an effigy of the New World is shown in the
orm of a giant sea-urchin surrounded by the orbit of an artificial satel-
ite. This version of the earth was confirmed by photographs relayed
rom a satellite.

The Battle of Tetuán, 1962, is another huge canvas, done especially
or the Gallery of Modern Art. As in most of his paintings, Dali fuses a
)hotographic precision of detail with surrealistic flashes. The great
)attle between the Spanish and the Moors took place at Tetuán in
Jorth Africa in 1860. The scene is a kind of poetic metaphor for the
essence of the battle, depicting the sensations of movement, noise,
ınd the splendour of colour.

The acting director is Miss Margaret Potter.

The museum is open Tuesdays through Saturdays 11 a.m. to 7 p.m.,
ɔundays and holidays 12 p.m. to 6 p.m. It is closed on Mondays.

31. (opposite above left) Sir John Everett Millais, The Huguenot, 1851
ıil on canvas $38\frac{7}{8} \times 25\frac{5}{8}$ in. (94×65 cm.)

32. (opposite above right) Sir Edward Coley Burne-Jones, The Doom Fulfiled,
884–88 oil on canvas $61\frac{5}{8} \times 55\frac{1}{2}$ in. (156·5×141 cm.)

33. (opposite below left) Gustave Moreau, Salomé Dancing before Herod, 1876
ıil on canvas $56\frac{3}{4} \times 40\frac{3}{4}$ in. (144·1×113·5 cm.)

34. (opposite below right) Salvador Dali, The Discovery of America by
:hristopher Columbus, 1959 oil on canvas $161\frac{1}{2} \times 122\frac{1}{8}$ in. (414×311·5 cm.)

Whitney Museum of American Art

945 Madison Avenue at 75th Street
IRT Subway (Lexington) 77th Street Station

85 In its relatively short history, the Whitney Museum of American A
has had quite a chequered career. It always was and still is a revolu
tionary force in American art, the latest contribution being a radica
new building designed by Marcel Breuer and opened in the autum
of 1966. With its stark unpolished walls of 'flamed' grey granite, th
monolithic cantilevered presence grows out over Madison Avenu
with one large trapezoidal eye exposed to the western sun. On th
75th Street side a group of these same curious reptilian eyes, posi
tioned assymetrically, relieve the monotony of the flat wall as the
reach out for light, creating triangular shadows of various sizes.

The building is a masterpiece of functional design as well as
serious attempt to create a mature structure expressive both of th
sincerity of the art that it houses, and of the vital exchange betwee
the artist and the public which has always been one of the Whitney'
chief aims. It provides three times the space of the previous building
with new innovations in lighting, moveable wall partitions, and
86 sunken sculpture garden for large, hard to move pieces.

The history of the Whitney is inextricably involved with the dramati
story of the evolution of American Art in the 20th century. During th
last third of the previous century American Art was under the spell o
19th century idealism. It lacked any direct confrontation with th
values and forces that were shaping a huge industrial nation
mechanization, sex, dirt, excitement, noise, large buildings and speed
American artists had virtually ignored every artistic innovation since
Impressionism. At the turn of the century the American art world wa
dominated by a thoroughly academic mentality—museums wer
nearly all historical; young non-academic artists had virtually no plac
to exhibit or sell their work.

In 1908 this Edwardian dream was invaded by the then scandalou
paintings of city life by Robert Henri and the Eight who painted slums
the Bowery, prostitutes, sailors and tenements with wash flapping i
the breeze. It was at this crucial moment in the history of American Ar
that Gertrude Vanderbilt Whitney, a wealthy sculptor with a studio or

85. (left) The Whitney Museum of American Art. 86. (right) The outdoor sculpture garden beneath the entrance bridge leading to the lobby of the museum

Macdougal Alley in Greenwich Village, then the heart of the new movement, began her life-long dedication to the innovatory forces in American Art. A good friend of Robert Henri and of Arthur Davies, two leaders of the Eight, Mrs Whitney bought four paintings from their first exhibition. She gave her support to the Madison Gallery where the idea for the Armory Show was spawned, and in 1914 she opened her own Whitney Studio at 8 West Eighth Street, next door to her sculp- ture studio. Then in 1915, with the energetic help of Mrs Juliana Force, she formed the Friends of the Young Artists; and in 1918 she opened the Whitney Studio Club at 147 West Fourth Street. The pur- pose behind all of these was the encouragement of new talent and the exhibition and sale of the works of young and unknown artists. No aesthetic credo was imposed and thus the club became a friendly meeting place for young artists—among the earliest were Sloan, Prendergast, Hopper, and Stuart Davis. It was from the exhibitions at the Club that Mrs Whitney made the selections that were to form the core of the present museum's collection.

By 1928, through her pioneering achievements, Mrs Whitney had

gained recognition for numerous young artists, and Modern Art wa
no longer an obscene expression in polite company – the Whitne
Studio Club had largely achieved what it set out to do. In 1931, wit
Mrs Force as director and a staff composed entirely of artists, th
Whitney Museum of American Art opened its doors on West Eight
Street. In 1954 it moved uptown next door to the Museum of Moder
Art on West 54th Street, where it remained until 1966.

Along with the important showings of works from the permaner
collection, and the publication of excellent accompanying catalogue
the Whitney's most significant contribution is the Annual Exhibitio
which attempts to show a fairly accurate cross-section of contempo
ary talent in the United States. Following in the tradition establishe
by the Friends of the Young Artists back in 1917, no prizes are awarc
ed and no jury chooses the 'best' painting or sculpture. Instead, th
Whitney purchases the works it likes, hoping in this way to give th
artist psychological as well as financial encouragement.

In the 1930's the Whitney was the headquarters for the fir:
governmental art programme – the Public Works of Art Project. I
1942, together with thirty other museums and college art department
it set up the American Art Research Council to make complete recorc
of the works of American artists in an attempt to discourage forgerie

With the opening of the new building in 1966 the museum bega
to re-establish its historical collection of works dating before 190(
most of which had been sold in 1949. The present permanent co
lection contains about 26,000 paintings, sculptures, prints and draw
ings, ranging from works by the Eight to the immediate present.

When academic artists labelled the Eight 'apostles of ugliness' the
87 surely had in mind paintings like John Sloan's *Backyards, Greenwic
Village*, 1914, with its neighbourhood kids and cats playing in th
snow, while Monday's wash hangs on a piece of rope stretche
between buildings. Another member of the group, George Luks, pos
sessed a remarkable ability to capture the essence of a personality wit
the greatest economy of means as is evidenced in *Mrs Gamley* c
1930.

George Bellows' style is close to that of Luks, especially in his us
of light almost as an element of abstract design. His famous *Dempse
and Firpo* was painted the year before his death, in 1924. The scen
shows Louis Angel Firpo, champion of South America knocking Jac
Dempsey, world heavyweight champion, clear out of the ring into
group of reporters (which included Bellows), who quickly shove
Dempsey back to win the fight by a knockout in the next round.

57. John Sloan,
Backyards, Greenwich Village, 1914
oil on canvas
26×32 in. (66×81·2 cm.)

All the significant pioneers of American abstract painting are represented in the Whitney. Arthur Dove's *Plant Forms* of 1915 done in
pastel is a kind of worm's eye view of motifs drawn from nature and
placed together in combining and overlapping areas. His *Ferry Boat
Wreck* – done as late as 1931 – shows his continuing preoccupation
both with natural forms and with near abstraction.

Along with Dove, Max Weber (b. 1881) was one of the first important American painters to be influenced by abstraction. His
Chinese Restaurant was perhaps the most adventuresome semi-
abstraction up to the time it was painted in 1915. As a celebration of
that venerable American institution – the Chinese restaurant – the
painting reflects Weber's own mood when he entered and was struck
by shapes of objects, movement, and splintered light reflecting from
coloured surfaces in a kaleidoscopic manner. The angular distortions
reflect Cubism while a sequence of overlapping faces and other forms
recalls the dynamic vibrations of Futurism.

As a youth in New York City, Lyonel Feininger (1871–1956)
acquired a fascination for the architectonic shapes of tall buildings
and the functional designs of machinery, which links him with the
Precisionists. These interests he combined with an early and keen
understanding of music plus a love of Gothic architecture to produce
a series of 'Gelmerodas'. *Gelmeroda VIII*, done in 1921, is built in
mathematical progressions, like an organ chord. Impressed by the
simplicity of Bach's music, Feininger tried to simplify and unify his
composition as much as possible. An air of mystery surrounds the
prismatic forms as they shade one into another creating a sensitive
and balanced painting with a masterful understanding of space.

Georgia O'Keeffe was far more interested in the gentle geometry
of flowers than in the steel girders of modern skyscrapers. *The White*

Flower, 1931, reveals the wonder of natural structure through delicate shading of white into various tones of grey. It was painted six years after she became the second wife of Alfred Stieglitz whose photography was often concerned with attaining similar effects.

Joseph Stella (1877–1946), of all American modernists, came closest to the techniques of Futurism which, like Stella himself, was born in Italy. His *Brooklyn Bridge: Variation on an Old Theme,* 1939 has all the symmetry of a Renaissance panel painting – even to the inclusion of the customary predella scene at the bottom. Stella has created a eulogy in paint to one of the great monuments of modern engineering technology (declared a National Monument in 1964).

88

Charles Sheeler (b. 1883) painted *Architectural Cadences* in 1954. He had been one of the founders of Precisionist painting in the 1930's and in this late work he used the controlled technique of his early style to create a low-keyed patchwork of insubstantial rectangles based on the architecture of an industrial complex.

The Whitney has several paintings by the Regionalists Benton and Curry. Benton's *The Lord is My Shepherd,* 1926, recalls certain aspects of Van Gogh's *The Potato Eaters* (in Holland), but Benton's characters wear expressions of almost belligerent self-righteousness instead of the reverent humility implied by the sign above their heads which likens them to sheep, in accordance with Psalm 23. Somewhat more objectively treated is Curry's *Baptism in Kansas* of 1928 where a girl dressed in white is undergoing 'total immersion' baptism at the hands of a fiery white-haired preacher in a farmyard trough, while family and congregation bow their heads and sing hymns.

Works by Charles Burchfield include his wonderfully animated landscapes in watercolour, such as *An April Mood* and *Noontide in Late May* and his large oil, *Old House by Creek. Noontide in Late May* 1917, is expressive of Burchfield's best style, to which he returned in later life. Trees and clouds, grass and fence posts all seem to writhe with the restlessness of some inner force. As in the paintings of Edvard Munch, brush strokes combine to create visual metaphors for auditory sensations.

In paintings like *Early Sunday Morning,* 1930, and *Seven a.m.* 1948, by Edward Hopper, morning light creates oblique shadows while the emptiness is that of beginning and anticipation, not of desertion or disillusion. One feels a sense of permanence and stability, a dignified isolation without sentimental overtones.

Like many figurative painters of the 1920's and 1930's, Walt Kuhn was first a magazine illustrator. Recalling the impressive solidity of the

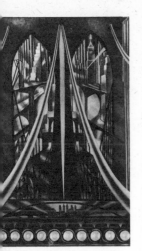 

8. (left) Joseph Stella, *The Brooklyn Bridge: Variation on an Old Theme*, 1939
il on canvas 70×42 in. (177·8×106·6 cm.)
9. (right) Reginald Marsh, *Why Not Use the 'L'?*, 1930
gg tempera on canvas 36×48 in. (91·4×121·9 cm.)

arly Cézanne, *The Blue Clown* of 1931 is a masterful composition
mploying a bold and effective use of colour. The tendency toward
bstraction seen in the face is countered by the taut muscles of the
eck, nose and lips, creating an over-all tension that bespeaks force
nd vitality in the personality of the sitter.

While the Regionalists were attempting to forge a national identity
ut of the myth of the American West — both legendary and contem-
orary — a group of New York artists including Reginald Marsh (1898–
954) and Raphael Soyer (b. 1899) were recording the hectic life of
he streets and subways of new York City. Marsh's *Why Not Use the* 89
'? of 1930 is one of his best paintings. The medium is egg tempera,
vhich allows for a more transparent surface than with oil. The triviality
f the sign (whose question the painting answers so well) and the
anality of the newspaper headline serve to underscore the vapid
xpression of the bespectacled girl at the right.

Soyer's *Office Girls* of 1936 has the appearance of a snapshot
aken almost at random in a crowd. The detailed attention given to
he painting of the girl's face who has been 'caught' by the brush
nakes her anonymity all the more poignant. A more compassionate
pproach is seen in *The Brown Sweater* of 1952 where a mother and
er two children in the background are painted 'out of focus' in order

90. (left) Ben Shahn, *The Passion of Sacco and Vanzetti*, 1931–32
tempera on canvas $84\frac{1}{2} \times 48$ in. ($214\cdot5 \times 121\cdot9$ cm.)
91. (right) Arshile Gorky, *The Betrothal, II*, 1947
oil on canvas $50\frac{3}{4} \times 38$ in. ($128\cdot9 \times 96\cdot5$ cm.)

to concentrate attention on the introspective face of a young woman
The artist shows a deep sympathy for and understanding of his sub
ject, one of many young tenement dwellers who spend long hours on
their front steps before nightfall.

One of the most avid and effective of the protest painters of the
1930's, Ben Shahn, has continued his battle against injustice an
90 hypocrisy to the present day. *The Passion of Sacco and Vanzett*
1931–1932, one of his earliest and most famous paintings, is a bitte
indictment of biased jurisprudence. During 1927, in the midst of a
anti-Red scare, Nicola Sacco and Bartolomeo Vanzetti, two Italia
immigrants, philosophical anarchists and minor labour leaders
were convicted of murder on scant evidence and sentenced to deat
by hanging. Because of the enormous public protest, the executio
was postponed several times, but finally in 1927 the verdict was con
firmed by a committee consisting of Lawrence Lowell, president o
Harvard, Samuel W. Stratton, president of M.I.T. and Judge Rober
Grant. Shahn painted the three men as they grimly pay their respect

to the two corpses. Ironically, the lilies they hold are symbols of life and purity. The great marble columns and steps of the courthouse behind them remind us of the power and impenetrablity of government institutions.

Philip Evergood (b. 1901) has given us a pathetic image of loneliness and poverty in *Lily and the Sparrows* of 1939. Following a personal vision bordering on the fantastic, a nearly hairless macrocephalic head rears itself with raised eyes from the open window of a red brick tenement, while brown sparrows hover in mid-air awaiting the crusts of bread offered in return for their cherished friendship.

Social comment in the 1950's became less vindictive than it had been in the 1930's, and Jack Levine's *Gangster Funeral,* 1952–1953, has lost the strong caricature present in the faces of his earlier works. Now a kind of modern folklore seems to pervade the scene where overdressed, overfed hoods attend the viewing of their dead colleague in an opulent setting replete with flowers, candles and a stained glass window.

The Betrothal II, 1947, by Arshile Gorky (1904–1948) was painted 91 during the artist's tragic last years when he was suffering from cancer —years that terminated in his own suicide. Gorky is one of the important forerunners of Abstract Expressionism. Here he has taken shapes reminiscent of Miró and Arp and combined them into a symbolic complex expressive of conflict, desire and fertility. His painting bears much in common with the obscure, forceful and often heavily erotic poetry of Dylan Thomas.

Stuart Davis (1894–1964), a friend of Gorky began studying with Robert Henri at the age of sixteen. At nineteen he exhibited in the New York Armory Show, and at twenty-seven he painted his famous *Lucky Strike,* one of the earliest paintings to assert the validity of commercial advertising as subject matter for the fine arts. The Whitney's *Owh! in* VII *San Pão* of 1951 is characteristic of Davis' witty celebration of light and colour, of the rhythms of modern city life with its signs, angular shapes and its endless strings of graffiti.

The sculpture collection contains examples of all major movements in America during the 20th century. Most of the heavier pieces are on display in the outdoor sculpture garden beneath the entrance bridge, 86 making a dramatic view for passers-by on Madison Avenue. Smaller works are to be found in the adjoining sculpture court or dispersed throughout the painting galleries.

The earliest and most powerful exponent of the new formal experiments at the beginning of the present century is Gaston Lachaise

(1882–1935). His *Standing Woman, 1912–1927* is a kind of earth mother, a great image of feminine sexuality whose energy is just barely contained within the lines of her body. In *Sacrifice II, 1948– 1952,* a prime example of Expressionist sculpture by Jacques Lipchitz (b. 1891), there is a clear reference to primitive religions and to the Abraham and Isaac story of the Old Testament. Natural forms are distorted in order to effect an extreme economy of means—a conciseness of statement with an electric impact. The very simplicity of William Zorach's *The Future Generation* is complimented by the intrinsic beauty of its pink Botticini marble, while Raoul Hague's *Sawkill Walnut* of 1955 takes inspiration from the aesthetics of pure form and revives traditional methods of working in wood.

A kind of baroque fantasy combined with modern expressionism is to be found in *Harp Player, II,* 1960, by Bernard Reder (1897–1963). The floating female figure flies at the strings with furious and explosive fingers becoming a three-dimensional metaphor for her own uncontained exuberance.

Theodore Roszak (b. 1907), like Lipchitz and Picasso, responded to the violence of world events by moving away from the smooth rectilinearity of his early works and into a semi-representational world of symbolic forms—claws, beaks, teeth and thorns. *Sea Sentinel,* 1956, uses the rough surface of brazed and pockmarked steel to add to the violence of its spidery, crab-like shapes that seem to be a reminder of elemental undersea forces. In a similar style and medium is *Sun Wheel* of the same year by Herbert Ferber (b. 1906). This 'free form' work, Ferber says, attempts to animate the space described by the choice of appropriately chosen shapes, which in turn create excitement and tension both real and suggested.

Calder's *The Cock's Comb,* 1960, is made from painted sheet aluminium, employing the technique of airplane construction (welded and riveted aluminium) to translate curved shapes resembling those of Arp and Miró into three dimensions. David Smith is perhaps the most important innovator after Calder. His *Hudson River Landscape* of 1951 is a kind of drawing in air with steel—as though the atmosphere were a two dimensional surface and steel were fluid like paint.

In her *Women and Dog* of 1964, Marisol (b. 1930) uses the products and by-products of mass technology—hats, ribbons, a dog collar, shoes — to create a curious *tableau vivant* of 'everyday people'.

The director of the museum is Lloyd Goodrich.

The museum is open every day from 11 a.m. to 5 p.m.; 12 p.m. to 6 p.m. Sundays; closed Christmas Day.

The Pierpont Morgan Library

29–33 East 36th Street at Madison Avenue
IRT Subway (Lexington) 33rd Street Station

The Pierpont Morgan library began as a serious hobby of the famed American industrialist John Pierpont Morgan (1837–1913). By 1905 Mr Morgan's private collection had grown to such a size that he commissioned the firm of McKim, Mead and White to build the now famous 'palazzo' next to the Morgan residence on 36th Street. The library is one of the most important centres for scholarly research in the humanities in America. It contains illuminated and textual manuscripts from the 6th to the 16th century, including the Constance Missal, a Gutenberg Bible on vellum and original autographed manuscripts by Keats, Byron and Dickens. One of the most outstanding possessions is the section of the *Hours of Catherine of Cleves*, a Dutch 15th century illuminated manuscript of exceptional beauty and historical importance. There are also book bindings from the 8th century to the present, master drawings from the 14th through the 18th century, and over 270 etchings by Rembrandt. Assyrian and Babylonian seals, cylinders and cuneiform tablets, and Egyptian, Greek and

92. The Pierpont Morgan
Library

139

other papyri are included also. There are also changing exhibits of various types.

The permanent collection of art on display in the West Room, which was Mr Morgan's study, is open to the public Tuesday, Thursday and Saturday. The room is arranged in the way Mr Morgan left it, and is therefore an important document in the history of taste as well as in the history of art. Paintings in the room include a 14th century altarpiece from Catalonia in Spain that has much in common with Sienese work of the same period, and two Bohemian panels from *c.* 1400, *The Adoration of the Magi* and *The Death of the Virgin.* From the hand of Hans Memling (d. 1494) come two wings of a triptych and the famous *Man With a Pink.* Also from the 15th century is Perugino's *Virgin and Two Saints Adoring the Child, c.* 1495, and two workshop pieces of Botticelli and Giovanni Bellini. From the 16th century there are two small circular wedding portraits of *Martin Luther and his wife,* 1525, by Lucas Cranach the Elder (1472–1553). Cima da Conegliano's *Mystic Marriage of St Catherine, c.* 1510, shows the mark of the Venetian school and the influence of Giovanni Bellini. Francesco Francia (*c.* 1450–1517/1518) was a goldsmith from Bologna whose *Virgin and Child with SS Dominic and Barbara, c.* 1500, shows the softening influence in his later work of the style of Perugino and Raphael. From the shop of the great 16th century Venetian Tintoretto comes the *Portrait of a Moor,* a popular subject often treated by Renaissance and Baroque artists. The small portrait on the easel is thought to be Marguerite de Valois, wife of Henry of Navarre, and may be placed in the circle around François Clouet (d. 1572).

93. (left) General view of the study

94. (opposite right) The New York Public Library
95. (opposite far right) Asher B. Durand, *Kindred Spirits,* 1849 oil on canvas 46×36 in. (116·8×91·4 cm.). The New York Public Library

Sculpture in the room includes a small statuette of *John the Baptist* which has been attributed to the early style of Michelangelo. A very lovely marble bust of a young woman, perhaps Marietta Strozzi, seems to be from the workshop of the Florentine follower of Donatello, Desiderio da Settignano (1428–1464). On the opposite side of the fireplace is a bust of a young woman usually attributed to another of Donatello's Florentine followers and the teacher of Leonardo, Andrea del Verrocchio (*c.* 1435–1488). Antonio Rossellino (1427–*c.* 1479) was also a pupil of Donatello whose softer style can be seen in the marble *Virgin and Child*.

The most important gold and enamel work is the famous *Stavelot Triptych*, a portable altar made by Godefroid de Claire about 1150 for Wibald, Abbot of Stavelot. It is an excellent example of 12th century Mosan work, comparable to the plaques from the same atelier at the Metropolitan Museum. The altar was made to house older Byzantine enamels which in turn frame fragments of the True Cross. The round medallions in the wings of the triptych are Flemish and show the *Conversion of Constantine to Christianity* and the legendary *Finding of the True Cross* by his mother, the Empress Helena.

Reproductions, slides, postcards and books may be purchased at the sales and information desk on the main floor.

The director is Frederick B. Adams.

The library is opened weekdays 9.30 a.m. to 5 p.m. and is closed on Sundays and holidays. It is also closed on Saturdays in July and the entire month of August. The Reading Room itself is opened only to qualified adults.

The New York Public Library

Fifth Avenue and 42nd Street
IND Subway (D train) 42nd Street Station; IRT
Subway (Lexington) 42nd Street Station, all subways
stopping at Times Square

94 The central branch of the New York Public Library System is housed
in the architectural masterpiece of John M. Carrère and Thomas
Hastings who also built the Frick mansion. The building is a triumph
of the French Beaux-Arts style of classicism, managing to keep a light,
airy quality in spite of its massive façade that dominates an entire
block along 5th Avenue. It offers changing exhibitions of prints,
drawings, lithographs, books, manuscripts, maps, stamps and paintings. The permanent collection of paintings is mostly contained in the
Berg Collection room. There are notable works by John Singleton
Copley and Gilbert Stuart. Changing exhibitions of prints, drawings
and lithographs are shown on the walls of the third floor halls.
Opposite the main reading room on the third floor hangs Asher B.
95 Durand's *Kindred Spirits*, 1849, which illustrates the close connection
between the artist and Thomas Cole, who is standing on the rock
along with the American poet, William Cullen Bryant. Cole was the
principal exponent of the Hudson River school of landscape painting
and Bryant's poetry is alive with the keen observation of nature that is
found in the painting of Cole and especially Durand. The Art and
Architecture room (313) on the third floor, along with the Donnell
branch of the New York Public Library System at 23 West 53rd Street,
comprises one of the best art reference libraries in the City. Many of
the library's holdings (manuscripts, prints, drawings, etc.) are not on
view to the public and permission to see them must be obtained from
the director's office.

The library is open weekdays from 9 a.m. to 10 p.m. and on Sundays
and holidays from 1 p.m. to 10 p.m. A book and card shop is located
in the lobby.

See pictures on page 141

The New York Historical Society

70 Central Park West at 77th Street
ND Subway, 81st Street Station

One of the most interesting places in the city to visit, and one of enormous import for anyone interested in American History and the artefacts pertaining to it, is the New York Historical Society. Changing exhibitions are organized on specific themes, areas, or persons. There are permanent collections of paintings, silver, glass, woodwork, furniture, early American toys, and the original 'Elephant Folio' of James John Audubon's *Birds of America* with 460 of the original watercolour drawings from which the plates for the volume were engraved.

The collection of American silver on the first floor begins with the 'pine tree shilling' struck in 1652 by John Hull and Robert Sanderson in Boston, and goes through the 18th and 19th centuries, including examples of candlesticks, dinner and tea services, trays, etc. On the same floor, the Waldron Phoenix Belknap collection of American portraits is one of the largest in the country, and paintings from it are shown along with examples of silver.

On the second floor are several rooms furnished in 17th and 18th century styles respectively. Important paintings include the famous *De Peyster Children* by an unidentified New York artist working in the 96 1720's and 1730's, and works by John Smibert (1688–1751) and Jeremiah Thëus (*c.* 1719–1774). There is a large collection of handmade toys, 18th–19th century New York stoneware pottery, Pennsylvania German red clay pottery painted in the traditional folk pattern and glazed, plus a large display of American glassware and bottles. Pewter used in homes and inns in the East makes an interesting addition to the silver which was used only by the wealthy or on special occasions.

The third floor contains a large and fascinating collection of early American arts and crafts. Duncan Phyfe's own tools are shown along with numerous examples of American folk art, most notably the Cigar Store Indians which once graced store fronts all over the country, and the colourfully painted boxes of the Pennsylvania Germans. In the gesso and polychrome techniques used, they are a prime example both of the direct carry-over of medieval craft traditions into this country and of the continuity of style among the products of untutored artists of all ages. Displayed along the walls of this floor is a large collection of American primitive paintings of the 17th, 18th and 19th centuries, revealing strong connections with the English portrait tradition, but unquestionably American in the treatment of landscape and in the often rude simplification of design and details.

The Bella C. Landauer Collection of letterheads, posters and broadsides brings back the styles and moods of days gone by in a remarkably vivid and often very humorous way. In these advertising posters addressed to the public at large, the virtues and follies of one generation are preserved marvellously intact for the appreciation and edification of the next.

The fourth floor contains more early American paintings, including Rembrandt Peale's *Portrait of Jefferson*, Charles Willson Peale' group portrait of the *Peale Family*, a Gilbert Stuart portrait of *George Washington*, the only known life portrait of *Peter Stuyvesant* and the two early 18th century portraits of *Thomas and Mrs Van Alstyne*, the latter having two right hands! Thomas Cole's dramatic series *The Course of Empire*, 1836, and paintings by John Durand and John F. Kensett as well as an important collection of early Italian paintings notably the large altarpiece of Nardo di Cione, are also on view.

Special events and services include an extensive educational programme featuring concerts, films, publications, guided tours, high school loan exhibitions, folk music and puppet shows.

The director is Dr James Heslin.

Books and pamphlets are available at the information desk on the main floor. The Society is open weekdays and Sundays from 1 p.m. to 5 p.m., Saturdays 10 a.m. to 5 p.m. It is closed Mondays, holidays and the entire month of August.

96. (opposite) Anonymous New York artist, *De Peyster Boy with Dog*, 1720–30 oil on canvas $50\frac{1}{4} \times 41$ in. ($127 \cdot 6 \times 104 \cdot 1$ cm.)

Museum of the City of New York

Fifth Avenue between 103rd and 104th Streets
IRT Subway (Lexington) 103rd Street Station; Fifth Avenue
Buses 2, 3, 4

The museum is dedicated to the illustration, through exhibits, of the history of the City of New York. It was originally housed in Gracie Mansion (now the residence of the Mayor), but moved in 1932 to the present Georgian style building, erected especially for it. Exhibits include the Dutch Galleries, where the history of New Amsterdam and its European background is explained by models and maps, and the Altman Foundation Gallery, which treats of life in the City from 1800 to the present, including a stage coach of 1855 and a horse-drawn ambulance of the early 1900's. In the first floor corridor are examples of early 19th century furniture, including some pieces by Duncan Phyfe. The portraits of Alexander Hamilton and his wife are by John Trumbull (1756–1843) who may be regarded as the great painter of the American Revolution. His dictatorial policies as head of the American Academy of the Fine Arts led to the resignation of several of its members and resulted in the formation of the National Academy of Design. A student of Gilbert Stuart, but quite opposed to the Stuart tradition in portraiture, Ralph Earl (1751–1801) was the best of the Connecticut painters of his time. The stiff, patterned and linear compositions are a hallmark of the American Puritan tradition in colonial portraiture. Matthew Pratt (1734–1805) was a follower of West in London who returned to America just prior to the Revolution, as did another of West's pupils, Charles Willson Peale. Pratt's portrait of *Mary Matlack* is charming, but it lacks the deep and subtle psychological insight with which Peale portrayed her husband, *Timothy Matlack*, in the National Gallery in Washington.

On the second floor there are several portraits by Gilbert Stuart (1755–1828), among them one of *George Washington* illustrating Stuart's fresh, quick approach with colours applied separately on the canvas. John Wesley Jarvis (1780–1840) was considered the best portraitist in New York in 1810. He was a tremendously prolific paint-

VIII. John Singleton Copley, *Midshipman Augustus Brine*, 1782
oil on canvas 50×40 in. (127×101·6 cm.). The Metropolitan Museum of Art

er, to the tune of six portraits a week at his peak. He was also New
York's first true Bohemian, a flamboyant and witty storyteller, a spend
thrift, an eccentric and a heavy drinker who was barred from polite fe
male company because of his debauched home life. The museum ha
several of his portraits, including the fine *Abraham Rodrique*
Brandon, a New York merchant. Joseph Badger (1708–1765), lik
many of the pre-Revolutionary homegrown artists, began as a hous
painter. He later rose to be the best portraitist in Boston after Feke unt
the rise of Copley. There are also portraits by John Durand and Charle
C. Ingham among others.

There is a large exhibition of New York silver also on the secon
floor, and two cases devoted to the Favrile glass of Louis Comfo
Tiffany (1848–1933). The vegetable-like shapes with long drooping
curves are characteristic of the Art Nouveau of 1900–1915.

On the same floor is the Marine Museum Gallery which contain
97 the famous sculptured figurehead of Andrew Jackson from the ol
U.S.S. Constitution.

The third floor has an exhibit of 18th and 19th century dolls and
toys, a 19th century drawing room with furnishings by Duncan Phyfe
and portraits by Rembrandt Peale and John Durand.

On the fifth floor are two furnished rooms from the John D
Rockefeller house that once stood at 4 West 54th Street. With the
original furnishings and mother-of-pearl inlaid rosewood and satin-
wood, they epitomize the elegance of Victorian taste.

Special events include the famous 'Sunday Walking Tours' of New
York City conducted by the historian Henry Hope Reed, Jr. Each tour
lasts about 2 hours and covers a particular section of the city. Tours
are given in Spanish also. The 'Please Touch' exhibits allow children
to handle 17th and 18th century household objects. There are concerts at 3 p.m. on Sundays from October to May, and puppet shows
and a puppet workshop for children on Saturdays.

The director is Ralph R. Miller.

Books, cards, reproductions, gifts and souvenirs are for sale on the
main floor. The museum is open Tuesday through Saturday 10 a.m.
to 5 p.m. and Sundays and holidays from 1 p.m. to 5 p.m. It is closed
Mondays.

97. (right) Figurehead of Andrew Jackson from the *U.S.S. Constitution*
wood height 118 in. (299·7 cm.)
The Museum of the City of New York

Asia House Gallery

112 East 64th Street between Park and Lexington Avenues
RT Subway (Lexington) 59th or 68th Street Stations

The gallery has no permanent collection. It sponsors loan exhibitions of Asian art and is closed for about one month between each exhibition. Distinguished specialists in the field are invited to select the works included in the exhibitions and to write accompanying catalogues. The building, designed by Philip Johnson, is faced with large slabs of opaque glass that allow light to penetrate, but preserve an element of privacy. There are seven floors, with a library and lounge on the first and a large exhibition area on the second. A 170 seat lecture hall occupies the basement. Other floors are taken up by the Japan Society and the Asia Society.

The director is Lionel Landry.

The gallery is open Monday through Friday 10 a.m. to 5 p.m., Saturdays 11 a.m. to 5 p.m., Sundays and holidays 1 p.m. to 5 p.m. It is advisable to contact the gallery in advance for information regarding current exhibitions.

New York City Hall

City Hall Park
IRT Subway (Lexington) Brooklyn Bridge Station;
BMT Subway (Local train) to City Hall Station

Aside from its importance as the seat of government of the largest city in the world, and its important collection of American paintings, the
98 City Hall is one of the finest surviving examples of public architecture in the Federal style (c. 1785–c. 1825). Completed in 1811, the building was designed by Joseph François Mangin in collaboration with John McComb. The Federal style, because of its connection with John Adams and the American Revolution, is often considered the most 'patriotic' of styles. It was a simplification of and a reaction to the Georgian style which preceded it and bore the unfortunate overtones of Georgian England. The City Hall gives us an example of the style not in its purest form, but influenced by buildings in France, for Mangin was himself a Frenchman. The interior is most remarkable for its double winding staircase with wrought-iron railings, which rises in an enveloping circle from the first floor to the second.

Most of the important paintings are on view to the public in three rooms, the Governor's Room, the Board of Estimate Room and the Council Chambers. The portrait of *Oliver Hazard Perry*, 1816, is one of a series of heroes of the war of 1812 that John Wesley Jarvis (1780–1840) did for the government. The rather theatrical poses of the figures and the mannerisms of Perry himself recall the bloated ego of the years after the war. Less pretentious, though more boring artistically, is the portrait of *Stephen Decatur*, 1814, by Thomas Sully. All the flags in New York harbour were hoisted to full mast and the bells made to ring for an hour at the reception of this war hero who commanded the ship *United States* in its decisive victory over the British ship *H.M.S. Macedonian* in October of 1812. Quite a different chap indeed was George Catlin (1796–1872) who left his home in Philadelphia to become one of the greatest painters of the frontier Indian, and whose book *North American Indians*, 1841, is an invaluable anthropological and ethnological record. Catlin was deeply involved in attempts to halt the injustices done to the southeastern tribes in the 1820's and 1830's. His portrait of *De Witt Clinton*, mayor of New York City, governor of New York state, and largely responsible for the con-

98. (left) The New York City Hall
99. (right) Samuel F. B. Morse, *The Marquis de Lafayette*, 1825–26
oil on canvas 96×64 in. (243·8×162·5 cm.)

struction of the Erie Canal, is a rarity done in 1827 while Catlin was in New York. Other paintings in the room include Henry Inman's full-length portrait of *President Martin Van Buren,* several works by John Trumbull including one of *Washington* and one of *Hamilton,* and paintings by Elliott and Vanderlyn.

In the Council Chambers is Samuel F. B. Morse's famous painting of the *Marquis de Lafayette,* 1825–1826. The great revolutionary 99 leader is portrayed in a manner commensurate with a character of grave dignity, a soldier of necessity and not of fortune. The difference between the spirit of 1876 and that of 1812 might well be summed up in the differences between this painting and Jarvis' one of Commodore Perry. The Board of Estimate Room contains paintings by Jarvis and Vanderlyn.

City Hall is open weekdays from 10 a.m. to 4 p.m. and closed Saturdays, Sundays and holidays.

Nicholas Roerich Museum

319 West 107th Street
IRT Subway (Broadway) 110th Street Station

The museum is dedicated to the dissemination of the ideals of art and culture which Nicholas Roerich, artist, philosopher, scientist and humanitarian devoted his life to achieving.

There is a permanent collection of paintings by Nicholas Roerich (1874–1947) and various objects from India, Tibet and the Himalayas. The works of other artists are featured in changing exhibitions of un-determined duration.

The extraordinary presence of the man, Nicholas Roerich, is every-where in the small converted town house. There are volumes of his poetry, descriptions of his paintings, biographies of him, articles by him and on him, but most extraordinary of all are his paintings. By no means do they rank among the greatest paintings of the 20th century, but for all their neo-medieval mystical romanticism, there is an ele-ment of truth in them, and one cannot but feel that the man who painted the nearly phosphorescent reds and blues, the lonely moun-tain peaks, the visionary saints and Madonnas was trying to say some-thing of importance.

Roerich was born in Leningrad, Russia, and studied law, art and history at the University there. Later he studied in Paris and travelled throughout Europe and Asia, especially Tibet. He painted stage de-signs for operas by Wagner, Rimsky-Korsakov, Ibañes, and Maeter-linck, and settings for 'Prince Igor' and 'Sacre du Printemps'. He painted over 6,000 paintings, published nearly thirty volumes, con-ducted archaeological expeditions to Central Asia, China and Mongo-lia. Perhaps his greatest achievement was the Roerich Pact which was signed by twenty-one nations in 1935, and over fifty by 1954. It was an agreement to respect all cultural sites and institutions in time of war.

The director is Mrs Nina Fosdick.

The museum is open daily and Sundays from 2 p.m. to 5 p.m. It is closed Saturdays, holidays and during all of July and August.

100. (opposite) The second floor showing paintings by Nicholas Roerich

Museum of Primitive Art

15 West 54th Street
ND Subway (E or F train) Fifth Avenue Station

The Museum of Primitive Art was opened in 1957 in order to give expression to a growing interest in the art of primitive peoples on both a scholarly and a popular level. About four exhibitions a year are shown, drawing on objects from the museum's own collection and from the collections of other museums as well as those of private individuals throughout the world. The museum includes two floors, is rather small and is air conditioned. Objects are intelligently and competently displayed. The scope of the exhibitions covers the native arts of Africa, Oceania, the Americas and pre-historic Asia and Europe.

The director is Dr Robert Goldwater.

A reference library on primitive art and culture is open by appointment from 1.30 p.m. to 5 p.m. Monday through Friday. The museum is open Tuesday through Saturday 12 p.m. to 5 p.m. and Sundays from 1 p.m. to 5 p.m.

Riverside Museum

310 Riverside Drive at 103rd Street
IRT Subway (Broadway) 103rd Street Station

The Riverside Museum, founded in 1938 by Mr and Mrs Louis L Horch, which is privately endowed, contains a permanent collection of Tibetan and Nepalese paintings and art objects on the second floor and a small collection of Japanese graphics and paintings in the entrance lobby.

The most important function of the museum, however, is its changing exhibitions of contemporary art, where one may gain a good idea of what is being done both in this country and abroad at the vanguard of activity. Past exhibits have included Women's Art from nine European countries, American abstract paintings, Contemporary Sculpture, and Pueblo Indian art.

The museum is affiliated with the Master Institute of United Artists which sponsors classes in the arts, music, and drama. One feels the sense of excitement and vitality of a school-orientated museum in the displays themselves and in the eager and interested people who often frequent the rooms.

The director is Mrs Nettie Horch.

The museum is open Tuesdays through Sundays from 1 p.m. to 5 p.m. It is closed Mondays, holidays and during the months of July and August.

Cooper Union Museum for the Decorative Arts

Cooper Square and Seventh Street
IRT Subway (Lexington) Astor Place Station

The Cooper Union is a philanthropic free enterprise established in 1859 by Peter Cooper, builder of the first American-made locomotive, the 'Tom Thumb'. The Cooper Union runs a free-tuition college of Art, Engineering, Architecture and Science and a Museum of Decorative Arts.

The building that houses the museum and classrooms is the first building in New York designed to be fireproof. It also contains the first elevator shaft which is circular and still in use. It was from the Great Hall of the Cooper Union that Abraham Lincoln delivered his famed pre-nomination speech on the extension of slavery in 1860.

The museum itself is primarily a research collection for students and designers. It has a permanent collection famour for its ancient and medieval textiles, drawings and prints from different periods including some by Dürer and Rembrandt, a large amount of wallpapers, ceramics, furniture, metalwork and costumes. Selections from the museum's large collection of works by Winslow Homer are often on display. The museum is particularly fun to visit for a change from the traditional display cases and wall hangings. You can walk through an 18th century wooden Venetian gate and stand in front of a fully lit Italian puppet show of the same period, complete with original costumes, strings, etc. There are also painted peep shows with early attempts at stereovision and trick lighting.

The director is Christian Rohlfing.

The museum is open weekdays from 10 a.m. to 5 p.m. and closed on major holidays, February 12, December 24 and 31 and on Saturdays from June 1 to October 1.

Museum of
Early American Folk Arts

49 West 53rd Street
same as for Museum of Modern Art

This is the youngest and the smallest of the City's museums, and for the foreign visitor it should be one of the more interesting, for it deals in the works of untutored American artists. The very idea of a museum dedicated to 'folk art' is a fairly recent development, since convention usually does not regard anything below the highest conceptual and technical standards as eligible to go by the delicate name of 'art'. The folk art of early America, however, is a genre unto itself, having more in common with the medieval traditions of Europe than with the academic traditions of the 18th and 19th centuries. In fact, there is an unbroken link between the folk art of Pennsylvania and that of Germany, between that of Salem and England, and New Mexico and Spain. The methods of late medieval artisans mixed with native traditions and were altered by the conditions and demands of a new environment to form an art at once vital and expressive.

If one judges American folk art by the critical standards properly applied to that produced by trained artists, no real understanding can result. The important things are the bold use of bright colours and the direct appeal to the mind and the senses by the shortest and least complicated route. This art was produced for the middle class by middle class artists and therefore carries the sentiment and the values of that group. It is due largely to the efforts of the descendants of these artists and their patrons that it has come into popular favour again.

The museum has a permanent collection which is not on display at all times, and holds loan exhibitions often supplemented by works from its own collections. It is the only museum in New York devoted exclusively to American folk art, from furniture to graphics.

The director is Mary Childs Black.

The museum is open Tuesday through Sunday, 10.30 a.m. to 5.30 p.m.

101. (opposite) An altarpiece from the Colorado Springs Fine Arts Center and Taylor Museum exhibited in the recent exhibition 'Santos, the Religious Folk Art of the American Southwest'. The Museum of Early American Folk Arts

154

The Museum of Contemporary Crafts

29 West 53rd Street
IND Subway (E or F train) Fifth Avenue Station

The Museum of Contemporary Crafts is operated by the American Craftsman's Council and is dedicated to exhibiting the work of contemporary craftsmen from all over the world. By showing objects made for everyday use which subscribe to the highest technical and artistic standards, the museum plays an important part in the education of the public with regard to quality design, and acts as a stimulating force in contemporary craft design both in this country and abroad. The exhibitions are changing and are well conceived and displayed in a modern building which is open weekdays and Saturdays from 12 a.m. to 6 p.m. and Sundays from 2 p.m. to 6 p.m.

The director is Paul Smith.

The Brooklyn Museum

Eastern Parkway and Washington Avenue, Brooklyn
IRT Subway (Broadway) Brooklyn Museum Station

102   Without a daring architectural tour de force to lure the curious,
record-breaking annual budget, or a location on Manhattan's fashion
able upper East Side, nevertheless the Brooklyn Museum manage
surprisingly well. It is probably the least pretentious and most informa
large art museum in the area, and yet it carries on one of the mos
varied and useful programmes of any comparable institution. Beside
nearly an entire floor devoted to the largest and best permanent dis
play of Primitive Art in New York, an Egyptian collection only out
sized by the Metropolitan, and a permanent display of 18th and 19t
century American paintings that ranks with the finest, there are classe
for adults and children in painting, drawing, sculpture, ceramics, an
conservation of works of art. There are also concerts, films, lecture:
tours, folk dances, and solo recitals. One has always the feeling tha
the museum and its collection are dedicated to the needs of its publi
and not to the whims of its curators.

Only twenty-seven minutes by subway from midtown, the museun
contains a cafeteria and a most interesting and reasonably priced git
shop featuring a large assortment of original folk art from many part
of the world.

102. The Brooklyn Museum

The main museum, the Brooklyn Children's Museum, the Art
chool, the Brooklyn Academy of Music and the famous Brooklyn
otanic Gardens are all under the sponsorship of the Brooklyn
stitute of Arts and Sciences, established in 1843 partly by the
ealthy local distiller Augustus Graham. The museum itself was
rganized in 1884 and the present building with its large marble-
olumned porch was constructed with city funds in 1890. The West
Jing was designed by McKim, Mead and White and opened in 1897;
ere were other additions in 1905, 1907, and 1925. An art reference
brary is open to the public from 1 p.m. to 5 p.m. daily except Satur-
ays, Sundays and holidays. Behind the building is a collection of
andstone and brownstone sculpture and some metalwork assembled
om doomed New York buildings of the 1890–1910 era by the
nonymous Arts Recovery Society, many of whose members are
emselves anonymous!

The first floor of the building is devoted to a cafeteria, the gift shop
nd the art of primitive peoples of the Western Hemisphere, the
rooklyn Museum being one of the first institutions in the country to
how serious interest in such artefacts as objects of beauty as well as
f cultural interest. Ancient ceremonial jars of the Zapotec period from
axaca are covered with complicated geometric ornament, and the
onumental stone sculptures from Vera Cruz on Mexico's Gulf Coast
how representations of the great Aztec gods. The art of Costa Rica
renowned for its beautiful gold jewellery and ornament, exemplified
y a gold tarantula cast by the lost wax process. The large hollow head 103
erved as a bell; its delicate legs reveal the quality of workmanship
at make the piece one of the finest in the collection. The art of

03. (below left) Gold tarantula, pre-Spanish Costa Rica. 104. (below right) Painted
vhale mask; Kwakiutl Indian, Vancover Island wood length 81⅛ in. (206 cm.)

Panama is close to that found in Costa Rica, and is best seen in the numerous examples of painted pottery and hammered gold jewellery. From the northwestern coast of South America, in the Andes, come the earliest pottery on the continent, dating to 3000 B.C. and from the tribes along the northern tributaries of the Amazon and the Orinoco there is clothing decorated with the brilliant, luminous, and phosphorescent feathers of tropical birds; beautiful woven fabrics with designs in *appliqué* are from the Central Andes region.

The aboriginal art of North America is well represented with examples ranging from Alaska to Mexico. Most impressive are the wood

104   carvings from the Kwakiutl tribes of the northwest coast. The carved and painted gods Raven, Thunderbird and Killer Whale have moveable parts such as beak, wings and fins which add to the spectacle when the masks are worn during ceremonies. As an example of the enormous monumentality which the woodcarving of the northwest Indians could attain, the museum has on display a totem cut into three lengths, each one well over twelve feet in height. When in situ the totem would have towered more than forty feet above ground. On the section to the right, the god Beaver is recognizable by his large stylized teeth. Above, a large bird is shown with a crescent moon in his claws which may refer to a legend that credits Raven with having stolen the moon from God's box of prized possessions. The Nathan Sturges Jarvis Collection of Plains Indian Art contains some of the oldest and best documented pieces in any museum.

By far the most important sculpture in Africa is to be found in masks, and it is helpful to remember that aesthetic qualities were highly functional in terms of the utility of a religious object. A particularly well-made mask might be retained for generations because of its effectiveness, while others, less effective, might be quickly discarded. Some of the finest carvings come from the Senufo people on the Ivory Coast. The *Firespitter Mask* was used by a witch-doctor who expelled hot coals from it to scare away evil spirits before a ceremony was to begin. The Benin tribes near the mouth of the Niger River in Nigeria came into early contact with Portuguese sailors at the end of the 15th century. Two bronze pieces, the *Flute Player* and the *Portuguese Sailor* attest to the dexterity and technical excellence which the Benin achieved in metal casting. The Bakongo *Nail Fetish* or *Power Figure* in the Lower Congo River style was given magical powers by substances placed within it, then activated by medicine men. Such 'charged' figures could be petitioned for protection against evil forces or for the fulfilment of wishes. The small glass window in the abdomen

05. *Nimba* mask; Baga, French Guinea wood

nade the potion visible while the nails were driven in during the eremony. The huge wooden *Nimba* mask from Baga on the French 105 Guinea coast is the embodiment of the goddess of fertility and maternity, and is worn on the shoulders like a harness during initiation tes for youth. The Baga produced some of the largest and most mas-ive masks in all of Africa. In the large architectonic surfaces one is ware of the influence of the broad open areas of the Sudan plains, nd the flat, inscribed decoration on the head probably indicates the nfluence of Islamic art on the native sculptors.

One of the most magnificent pieces is the large initiation mask om the Sepik River area of New Guinea. It is carved with elong-ted and highly stylized features, painted black with white markings, nd topped with a small crown of feathers. The mask is remarkably ophisticated and highly developed in both design and technique.

The art of the Pacific Islands is represented by several exhibits, mong the most interesting are the Wayang puppets from Java. Early xamples were cutouts from buffalo hide whose movements were rojected on a translucent screen with light from a brass Garuda bird mp. Later the cutouts were elaborated into dolls and the translucent creen replaced by a stage so that the Wayang took on the appear-nce of a Punch and Judy show. The stylizations in the painted faces nd the sarongs of the puppets are unique, evoking the mood of ystery that still surrounds many of the magic ceremonies of the lands.

On the second floor are the newly installed Oriental galleries and e arts of India. The Print Department holds changing exhibitions which are especially strong in 19th and 20th century European and American works.

On the third floor is the Hagop Kevorkian Gallery of Ancient Middle Eastern Art with its twelve large alabaster slabs from the Northwest Palace of King Assur-Nasir-Pal II at Nimrud, 883–859 B.C. There are also examples of small statuary in stone and metal, along with jewellery and gold and silver-work.

The Egyptian collection is also on the third floor. It is particularly rich in later periods, especially Coptic, and along with the Charles Edwin Wilbour Memorial Library of Egyptology (on the same floor) it constitutes a major centre for scholarship on Ancient Egypt.

Some of the oldest sculptures are the small pottery figures of women with bird-like heads and long arms flailed above them. Made long before the invention of writing, their use can only be guessed at though most authorities agree that they served some religious function.

From Old Kingdom Egypt (end of the III Dynasty) the red granite head, probably King Kuny, is among the few early royal portraits existing outside Cairo, while the three small statuettes of King Pepy I and II are perhaps the best preserved of the few surviving royal statues of the VI Dynasty.

Several excellent carved limestone reliefs of the Middle Kingdom are fragments from a royal tomb depicting Queen Neferu's toilet preparation and demonstrating the Ancient Egyptian preoccupation with continuing the modes of the present world into the hereafter. Also from the Middle Kingdom (XII Dynasty), the small diorite statue of King Sesostres III, greatest of the Middle Kingdom rulers, no longer wears the serene expression of earlier portraits. He seems worried, his serious eyes aloof and heavy with the burdens of statecraft.

108   From the New Kingdom there is a large diorite head of Amenhotep III (XVIII Dynasty), which by its sheer size and the force of its carving dominates the gallery that houses it. The splendid wall decorations of the Amarna period can be sampled in the delicate *Antelope in Flight* c. 1365 B.C., modelled in low relief in limestone, an excellent example of its period and style.

From the early Ptolemaic period there is a gilded wooden sarcophagus for a sacred Ibex with tooled silver head and legs, c. 300 B.C. The ibex was sacred to Thoth, god of magic, medicine and learning. Remarkable for its unprecedented portrayal of the Emperor

IX. (opposite) Marc Chagall, *The Soldier Drinks*, 1912 oil on canvas 43 × 37¼ in. (109·2 × 99·6 cm.) The Solomon R. Guggenheim Museum

106. (opposite above) Francis Guy, *Winter Scene in Brooklyn, c.* 1817
oil on canvas 58¾×75 in. (149×190 cm.)
107. (opposite below) Edward Hicks, *The Peaceable Kingdom*
oil on canvas 17½×23¾ in. (44·4×60·3 cm.)
108. (above left) Amenhotep III, XVIII Dynasty diorite
109. (above right) River goddess; Coptic limestone

Alexander the Great is a small alabaster bust considered a true masterpiece of late Hellenistic art from Egypt, *c.* 200–150 B.C.

The period of Egyptian history during which time Egypt was a
Christian state, and the art it produced, is known as Coptic. Several
limestone relief sculptures from the 2nd through the 6th centuries
A.D. attest to the increasing abstraction and other-worldliness of
Coptic art. The survival of classical themes is demonstrated by a limestone portion of a ceiling made for Christian use showing a pagan
river god and earth goddesses; it is from the studios of Ahnâs, one of 109
the greatest centres of Coptic sculpture. Other pieces include a limestone arch (6th century A.D.) decorated with birds and plants, probably from a Christian church. The museum has several of the remarkable portraits from Fayyum in Upper Egypt. Painted in hot wax
(encaustic) on wooden panels, they were inserted in the mummy
wrappings over the head as a kind of mask. A variety of Coptic textiles
is also on display.

The fourth floor of the museum contains a large collection of
American and European decorative and practical arts. It also houses
twenty-five of the largest and most creatively arranged early American
furnished rooms in New York. Outstanding is the *Jan Martense
Schenck House,* one of the few surviving examples of 17th century

Brooklyn architecture. It was built in 1675 in a style distinctly Dutch but has only been restored to a date of about 1730.

Other exhibits on the same floor include American stoneware pottery, revival style American furniture from 1670–1840, European and American samplers, a display of American silver, pewter, metal work, Wedgwood, cameos, European ceramics, porcelain, early American toys, costumes, and prints of Audubon's *Birds of America*

On the fifth floor are European and American paintings and sculptures. The collection of European painting is small, but representative There are several 14th and 15th century Italian panel paintings Ribera's *St Joseph With the Flowering Rod,* Hobbema's *Hamlet in the Woods,* Géricault's *Study for Le Cuirassier Blessé,* Delacroix *Disciples at Emmaus;* and a number of works by Corot, Degas, Monet Monticelli, Morisot, Toulouse-Lautrec, Pascin, Pissarro, Utrillo Vlaminck, and Dufy, as well as a group of European watercolours.

The American paintings are outstanding by any standard, and a few of the 18th century portraits and 19th century landscapes are un surpassed anywhere.

110   *Deborah Hall,* 1766, by William Williams (d. *c.* 1790) is one of th most important of the small group of paintings surviving from th artist's hand. His painting of Deborah Hall attains a remarkable refinement and sensitivity in the face, while at the same time the improbable drapery folds and the elaborately impossible garden place the artist within a local native tradition. Deborah, in her lovely silk dress with its carefully painted lace sleeves, is more decorative than real, and her little pet squirrel (or is it a chipmunk?), in spite of it delicate chain and twirled silk cord, is as wild as the rose that grow in the out-of-perspective pot.

Of the many portraits of George Washington by Gilbert Stuart, th 'Lansdowne type' in the Brooklyn Museum has a particularly interest ing history. While Stuart was working on a standing portrait of Washington for a Mr Bingham (who was to give it to the Marquis of Lansdowne, hence the name) Mr William Kerin Constable of New York, a good friend of the artist, liked it so much that he commissioned Stuart to do another. In order that they both be considered 'original' the artist worked on them at the same time. This one, dated 1796, ha always been in the possession of Brooklyn families and is considered to be one of the most accurate likenesses of America's first president

Francis Guy (1760–1820) was an English immigrant who had been a tailor, a dyer, an oilcloth and carpet manufacturer, a dentist, a

106   poet, and a minister of the gospel. He painted *Winter Scene in Brook*

110. William Williams,
Deborah Hall (detail), 1766
oil on canvas
71¼ × 46½ in. (180·9 × 118·1 cm.)

yn about 1817, probably just after his return from Baltimore, where
he had done most of his painting previously. It is the best of all Guy's
work, recalling the elder Bruegel in its concern with anecdote and
detail. Guy worked from his window on Front Street, often calling to
his neighbours to stand still and 'don't move'. The mansions of the
wealthier Brooklynites can be seen in the right distance, while at
centre a chimney sweep emerges to wave at the painter.

One of the most extraordinary of all early American painters is
Edward Hicks (1780–1849), son of a Pennsylvania farmer. A man
both possessed and obsessed, he became an extreme Quaker and
gave up sign painting which he came to believe was a mere companion to indulgence, voluptuousness and pride. His passion drove
him to become an evangelical preacher, and he travelled throughout
the northern states and Canada delivering sermons. He never studied
art formally, believing education to be a diabolical device. Eventually
he went back to painting, but thought himself a failure and a good-
for-nothing. He is the classic American folk artist, self-appointed, self-
taught and self-publicized. He painted numerous *Peaceable King-* 107
doms which illustrate the prophesy of Isaiah that 'the wolf . . . shall
dwell with the lamb, and the leopard shall lie down with the kid; and
the calf and the young lion and the fatling together; and a little child
shall lead them.' Lest we miss the point, Hicks has interpreted the
allegory for us with a little scene on the left of a pow wow between
William Penn's Quakers and the Indians.

John Quidor (1801–1881), born at Tappan on the Hudson, a few
miles from New York City, is one of the most original painters of his
time. Like many another, he painted signs, banners, and fire engine
backs for a living. His only formal training consisted of a brief appren-

ticeship with John Wesley Jarvis, from whom he took little. His own romantic and humourously expressive style combined with his pre dilection for the stories of Washington Irving and James Fenimore
111 Cooper to produce a peculiarly native art. *Wolfert's Will* illustrates in dramatic fashion Irving's story of an old miser on his death bed who upon learning that the farm he has just bequeathed is to become enormously valuable, decides not to die after all!

The museum has a particularly fine selection of American land scapes. *The Morteratsche Glacier, Upper Engadine, Pontresina*, 1895 by Albert Bierstadt is a good example by the most impressive of the second generation of Hudson River painters. His technical compet ence is remarkable, and his rendering of vast space and monumental landscape to the minutest detail appealed to his patrons and made him an extremely wealthy man. Bierstadt's contemporary, Frederick E. Church, is the pictorial counterpart to Ralph Waldo Emerson, who had demanded that artists recreate nature by investing it with a hidden spirituality. *South American Landscape*, 1873, demonstrates Church's favourite trick of showing sunlight reflected from the dim face of water, filling a surface mist with golden light. George Inness (1825–1894) was a follower of the Hudson River School, but his *June*, 1882, recalls more the loose style of Corot and the French Barbizon painters whom he admired. The painting is of a serene pasture, perhaps along one of the tiny streams that run through New Jersey into the Delaware River. The velvety green grass and the somewhat fuzzy-edged trees are part of a perfectly balanced composition.

Ralph Blakelock (1847–1902) was committed to a mental institu tion in New York about 1899 and never painted again. His tragic life was marked by poverty, neglect and madness, and he was never able to realize the benefits of the popularity his paintings attained shortly
112 before his death. Most of them are very similar to his *Moonlight, c.* 1885. The colours recall Giorgione and the mood is only slightly less stirring. The technique is pasty and spotty, not brushed. The white light of the moon dimly illuminating the sky and reflecting from the water contrasts with and balances the reddish glow of the Indian campfire on the left.

Eastman Johnson (1824–1906) is one of the best American genre painters. While studying at The Hague he was known as the 'American Rembrandt'. The somewhat cluttered and heavy atmosphere of his *Not at Home*, 1865, almost attacks the olfactory nerves with the smells of a dimly lit Victorian interior where mid-century anecdotalism is coupled with a precise technique learned in Dusseldorf.

111. (left) John Quidor, *Wolfert's Will*, 1856
oil on canvas 27×34 in. (68·5×86·3 cm.)
112. (right) Ralph Blakelock, *Moonlight, c.* 1885
oil on canvas 27¼×32¼ in. (69·2×81·9 cm.)

William Merritt Chase (1849–1916) is more important for his
theories and his teaching than for his paintings. He became president
of the Society of American Artists and a teacher at the Art Students
League in New York. *The Artist's Studio,* 1880–1883, is a veritable
policy statement of the new movement, with its large collection of
European artefacts prized by Chase and his American patrons who together shared a desire to discard provincial attitudes and absorb
European culture, for which they paid gladly in American dollars.

In Philadelphia, toward the end of the century, there grew up a
tradition of illusionistic still-life based more on the earlier example of
Raphaelle Peale and his family than on the Dutch 17th century. The
greatest of these *trompe l' oeil* masters was William Harnett (1848?–
1892). His *Still-life,* 1880, attempts with photographic realism to
bridge the gap between art and life. John F. Peto (1854–1907) was
less a precisionist and his *Still-life With Lanterns,* 1890 or after, is
more lyrical in design and painterly in treatment.

Frank Duveneck (1848–1919) was, along with Chase, the chief
exponent of 'New School Realism' brought back from Munich where
he ran an art school for some years. The style of his delightful *Mary* 113
Cabot Wheelwright, 1882, derives as much from Velasquez and Goya
(cf. *Don Manuel Osorio de Zuñiga* in the Metropolitan, facing p. 49)
as from the French realists, Courbet and Manet. The pure, fresh colours
and the broad, open painting are perfectly suited to the innocence of
the subject.

113. (left) Frank Duveneck, *Mary Cabot Wheelwright*, 1882
oil on canvas 50×33¼ in. (127×84·4 cm.)
114. (right) Thomas Eakins, *William Rush Carving His Allegorical Figure of
the Schuylkill River*, 1908 oil on canvas 36×47¾ in. (91·4×121·2 cm.)

114   Thomas Eakins painted three versions of *William Rush Carving His
Allegorical Figure of the Schuylkill River*, which depicts the first important American-born sculptor, William Rush (1756–1833), carving
the commemorative monument for the inauguration of the new water
works which would make use of the water from the Schuylkill. Rush
chose for his model the daughter of Mr Vanuxem, a wealthy merchant
and a fellow member of the water committee. The realistic treatment
of the nude caused a scandal which had symbolic value for Eakins,
who had himself been forced to resign from the Philadelphia Academy
of the Fine Arts for requiring his female students to know *all* of the
male anatomy. Eakins' own picture was greeted with prudish frowns,
and in this later version of 1910, the female figure appears somewhat
more idealized than in earlier ones. Eakins made his painting as histori-
cally accurate as possible, even to the inclusion of the chaperone who
is shown knitting. He visited the sight of Rush's shop and obtained
descriptions of its interior from old timers and from Rush's own sketch
book.

Perhaps the best painting in the museum by a member of 'the
Eight' is William Glackens' *Nude with Apple*, 1910, though John
Sloan's *The Haymarket*, 1907, or George Luks' *Hester Street*, 1905,
are more revealing of the subject matter and style that won for the

group the name 'Ashcan School'. *Nude with Apple* is Glackens' masterpiece, the culmination of his numerous figure studies. The reclining nude is one of the most common motifs in the history of art; for recent examples one thinks immediately of Goya and Manet. Glackens was also a magnificent and daring colourist much influenced by Renoir. The paint is thick, applied wet into wet; the shoe on the couch is of such a dense purple and so heavily painted that it appears almost black, while the shades of red approach the infinite in number, and the flowers around the large straw hat are as pasty as roses on a birthday cake.

Charles Sheeler (1883–1965) was the most outstanding of a group of American artists known as the 'Immaculates.' His *Incantation*, 1946, shows, in its precise drawing and clinical treatment of forms, the results of both his own earlier abstractions and his work in photography. The tanks, pipes and valves of a refinery become the point of departure for a stylized hymn to modern industry and its functional shapes.

Larry Rivers (b. 1923) reveals a remarkable economy of means in his *July*, 1955. He paints not reality, but images of reality: a bicycle, an apron, the corner of a house; but the whole becomes acutely expressive of its title. A dull section of suburbia, lower middle class America in its own back yard, three generations are shown staring emptily and anonymously as though seen through the window of a passing car. Rivers ties the loosely organized parts of the composition together with a knowing balance of colours. It is what he leaves out that gives force to what he includes.

A tour is available of a special *Study Collection* of paintings between 1 p.m. and 4 p.m. on Wednesdays and Saturdays. It is opened at other times only by permission obtainable from the information desk on the main floor. Paintings are here shown on sliding and rotating panels, as is often done in commercial galleries. Many pictures previously doomed to storage are thus visible to the public for study.

Modern European and American sculpture contains among others, works by Seymour Lipton, Gaston Lachaise, Amedeo Modigliani, Leonard Baskin, William Zorach, Frederick MacMonnies, David Smith, and Elliot Offner. An excellent collection of works in bronze by the French sculptor Antoine-Louis Barye (1796–1875) is located with the European paintings.

The director is Thomas S. Buechner.

The museum is opened Mondays through Saturdays 10 a.m. to 5 p.m., Sundays and holidays 1 p.m. to 5 p.m.

Out of doors and incidental

The resources of New York as a world art centre are in no way exhausted by the city's several major repositories for painting and sculpture. In churches, public buildings and large corporations as well as in parks and squares there exists a vast and constantly growing treasury of art works. The architecture of the city itself offers a wide range of styles (many of them rapidly disappearing) – from the few remaining colonial houses to the towering walls of glass and steel that characterize Manhattan today. A good way to visit the city is from south to north, following its growth from a tiny Dutch settlement near the Bowery to the largest city in the world.

115 From Battery Park at the very tip of lower Manhattan one can take a boat ride to Liberty Island to visit the best-known piece of sculpture in America – Frederick Bartholdi's 225 ton figure of *Liberty Enlightening the World,* popularly known as the Statue of Liberty. Constructed of hand-hammered copper plates, and supported by an intricate skeleton of steel which is the work of Gustave Eiffel, Liberty is personified as a woman stepping from broken shackles. In her right hand is a torch, in her left a tablet with the Declaration of Independence and the date July 4, 1776, inscribed upon it. The monument was a gift from the French people (the money was raised by popular subscription) to the United States in commemoration of 'the alliance of the two nations in achieving the independence of the United States of America, and attests to their abiding friendship.' It was dedicated by President Grover Cleveland on October 28, 1886.

In Battery Park itself there are a few statues, interesting mainly for their historical associations. A three-quarter length figure of *Giovanni da Verrazano,* a Florentine navigator said to be the first to have entered New York harbour in 1524, rests on a granite pedestal. It was sculpted by Ettore Ximenes and donated by local Italians in 1909. In the north-western section is a flagstaff base with a stone relief statue of *Peter Minuit,* governor of New Amsterdam, who reputedly 'bought' the island from the Manhattoes Indians for a mere twenty dollars worth of goods. On the corner of Pearl and Broad Streets, northeast of the

115. The Statue of Liberty

Battery, is Fraunces Tavern, originally built in 1719. It was an active centre of life in 18th century New York, and the site of General Washington's farewell to his soldiers in 1783. The old building was first burned out in 1837 and nearly destroyed by fire again in 1852. The present building is a careful 1907 reconstruction that nevertheless affords a good likeness of late colonial architecture. A museum of revolutionary relics is on the third floor and a restaurant occupies the first. Further north, at the corner of Old Slip and Stone Streets (first paved street in New Amsterdam) is India House, a club for persons engaged in shipping and foreign trade. It has a fine collection of early prints, paintings and models of sailing vessels. Number 7 State Street is perhaps the city's best preserved example of Federal style domestic architecture with one of the handsomest early façades in New York. Originally the home of John Watson around 1800, the house is believed to have been built by John McComb who collaborated on the City Hall. The building (now the Mission of Our Lady of the Rosary) is notable for its tall white columns, its delicate ironwork balcony and its beautiful old handcarved mantlepieces.

At the end of lower Broadway in the shadow of towering concrete skyscrapers is the oldest public park in Manhattan, Bowling Green, built in 1733 as a place to play ninepins. At the south end is a bronze seated figure of *Abraham de Peyster*, mayor and acting governor of New York, in 18th century costume, sculpted by George Bissel around 1896.

Trinity Church on the corner of Broad and Wall Streets was design-ed by Richard Upjohn in 1846 in Gothic revival style. It is a beautifully proportioned building with an exceptionally fine tower. Of the three sets of bronze doors cast in base relief and resembling Ghiberti's doors to the Florentine Baptistery, the pair by Karl Bitter on the west portal is the finest. The stained glass, some of the oldest made in America, was fired on the spot—an innovation at the time—and in-stalled under Upjohn's own direction. The window above the main altar is of exceptional beauty.

Federal Hall National Memorial, on the corner of Wall Street and Broadway, is one of the first examples of Greek revival architecture in the city. It was designed in 1842 by Ithiel Town and Alexander Jackson Davis, famed designers of state capitals in the United States. On the steps, in front of the eight massive fluted columns, is John Quincy Adams Ward's masterpiece, the statue of *George Washington*, 1883, which stands on the very site where the general took the oath of office as first president of the United States in 1789. Inside are historical exhibits relating to George Washington and John Peter Zenger, who was instrumental in establishing freedom of the press in America.

St Paul's Chapel of Trinity Parish between Fulton and Vesey Streets on Broadway is the oldest remaining church building in Man-hattan. Its cornerstone was laid in 1764 by James McBean, a Scots-man and pupil of James Gibbs who designed St Martin's-in-the-Fields, London. The light, spacious interior with its gentle barrel vault on fluted Corinthian columns is particularly enjoyable. Against the west wall of the interior is a bust of *John Wells* (1770–1823) by John Frazee, reputed to be the first known portrait bust by a native American sculptor.

A little further north is City Hall Park with a statue of *Nathan Hale* by Frederick MacMonnies done in 1890, one of the better works by this New York sculptor. Hale wears the costume of a Dutch school teacher, the disguise under which he entered the British lines, and in which he was executed as a spy. Around the handsome pedestal by Stanford White are inscribed the famous words Hale spoke before his death. The City Hall itself is discussed on page 148.

From the steps of the City Hall one can see the famous Brooklyn Bridge designed in 1867 by John A. Roebling with its huge buttressed towers of granite, its Gothic pointed arches and its web of steel cables spanning the East River. Much of the visual effect of the bridge derives from the contrast between the compression in the towers and the tension of the steel members. On the right, at Broadway and Park Place is the Woolworth Building erected in 1913 by Cass Gilbert. The first 'Cathedral of Commerce,' its soaring Gothic walls were for many years the tallest in the world. By shifting emphasis from concealed to revealed structure and by departing from weight and mass to atmospheric lightness, Gilbert made an important contribution to the American skyscraper style. All the details are Gothic; there are even flying buttresses.

The oldest cathedral in the city, St Patrick's Old Cathedral (not to be confused with St Patrick's on Fifth Avenue) is at 263 Mott Street, near Houston Street. Inside, the columns are of gilded cast iron and the ceiling is painted stucco, all done in a true medieval fashion. Located as it is in the Italian section of Manhattan, the interior with its hundreds of candles and plaster of Paris statues provides an atmosphere perhaps more European in feeling than any other church in the city. One of the earliest examples of the Gothic revival, it is supposed to have been designed by Joseph François Mangin in 1809–1815.

The Old Merchant's House at 29 East 4th Street in Greenwich Village, in fairly dilapidated condition, was built in 1832 in red brick Greek revival style. The richly decorated interior contains examples of Duncan Phyfe's furniture (his factory on Fulton Street was not far away). The house is now open as a museum.

West of Broadway is Washington Square, with its Greek revival houses along Washington Square North known as 'The Row'. Now the offices of New York University, whose buildings surround the Square, these lovely red brick houses with white limestone trim have been the homes of numerous artists and writers including Henry James, who named a book after the Square. Stanford White's famous Washington Arch built in 1895 as a gateway to Fifth Avenue stands alone on the Square's north side, framing the large circular fountain and N.Y.U.'s new chapel in the background. It commemorates the first inauguration of George Washington who is represented by two monumental marble panels as commander-in-chief and as president, on the left and right respectively. Across the park from the Arch is Judson Memorial Baptist Church constructed of amber-coloured brick with a slender Lombard campanile by Stanford White. Twelve of the stained glass windows were designed by the American painter John La Farge (1835–1910).

116. St Mark's-in-the-Bouwerie

A number of works of art are owned by New York University itself and are on display in the Loeb Student Center on Washington Square South and in various parts of the University throughout the city.

The Church of the Ascension designed by Richard Upjohn in English Gothic style in 1841 and redecorated by Stanford White in 1888 is located on the corner of Fifth Avenue and 10th Street. It contains a large mural of the *Ascension* considered to be John La Farge's finest work. Many of the excellent stained glass windows were also made after designs by La Farge.

116 At Second Avenue and 10th Street is one of the oldest buildings in Lower Manhattan, Ithiel Town's Church of St Mark's-in-the-Bouwerie (which means St Mark's in the farm, after Peter Stuyvesant's farm on which the original Dutch Chapel was erected in 1660). The present building with its cast iron portico was built during 1795–1799. The tower and steeple were added later. The reredos behind the altar is by Chester Beach, a pupil of Rodin, and the windows were copied after designs in William Blake's *Book of Job.*

The little Grace Episcopal Church at the corner of Broadway and 10th Street designed by James Renwick, who also designed St Patrick's Cathedral on Fifth Avenue, is often considered the finest example of Gothic revival in the city. The wood carving on pews and on mahogany choir stalls is some of the best in New York.

At the intersection of Greenwich Avenue, West 10th Street, and Sixth Avenue, is Jefferson Market Court, now a branch of the New York Public Library. It was designed in part by Calvert Vaux, 1876, in fantastic Victorian Gothic with weird turrets, traceried windows and carved stone. This exceptional and imaginative gem with a ten-story clock tower was noted as one of the ten most beautiful buildings in the United States in a survey of 1876. It was saved from demolition only after a three year fight by residents of Greenwich Village.

Louis Sullivan's only edifice in New York is the Condict Building, 1898, at 65 Bleeker Street (near Lafayette). Though a minor example of his work, it affords a good showing of his rich and inimitable ornament on the façade.

At 66 West 12th Street, the New School for Social Research has frescoes and murals by Thomas Hart Benton, Camilo Egas, and the only Orozco murals in New York. The Benton frescoes, in a classroom on the fifth floor, are perhaps the best of the lot. They represent a cross-section of American life in all its social, industrial and intellectual intensity. It was this colourful, vigorous style with its inclusion of machine parts, workmen, locomotives, and steel mills that dealt a final blow to the dying idealist school which flourished at the turn of the century. The Orozco murals are stark condemnations of militarism and bureaucracy.

In Union Square between Broadway and Park Avenue and 15th and 16th Streets, famous as a centre for lively open-air debates, there are statues of *Lincoln* and *Washington* by Henry Kirke Brown (1814–1886), one of the first American sculptors to reject the accepted proposition that a successful career must begin with study in Italy. In the centre of Grammercy Park at Lexington Avenue and 20th Street is a statue of *Edwin Booth* by Edmond T. Quinn. He is shown in his best-known role as Hamlet. Nearby is the famous Players Club where Booth spent many hours practicing and studying. Numbers 3 and 4 Grammercy Park are decorated with beautiful cast iron railings, presenting one of the most attractive façades in Manhattan. A little farther east on 20th Street at Number 28 is the Theodore Roosevelt birthplace now opened as a museum. It is one of the few well-preserved brownstones left, with an interior maintained as it was over a century ago.

Perhaps the most famous building in New York, and still the tallest, is the Empire State Building between 33rd and 34th Streets on Fifth 94 Avenue. Opened in 1931, it is a lasting monument to the boom years between 1924 and 1929. The pattern of window, spandrel, window,

spandrel is repeated for 755 feet without interruption, in direct contrast to earlier skyscrapers where each story is marked by a horizontal
cornice. The building's continuous wall surface with flush-set windows serves to emphasize the enormous height (1,250 feet) and in-
vites the eye to soar up with unbroken speed. From the observatories
on the 86th and 102nd floors one can see a 50 mile panorama of New
York and its suburbs on a clear day.

The most famous architectural ensemble in Manhattan is Rockefeller Center where architecture, sculpture, mural painting and metalwork combine in an impressive complex. The most conspicuous works
of art include Paul Manship's great gold *Prometheus* against the west
wall of the plaza. The interior walls of the R.C.A. building are covered
with murals by José Maria Sert in a very effective brown monotone
representing Man's accomplishments through the union of physical
and mental labour. The 45 foot bronze *Atlas* by Lee Lawrie looking
down Fifth Avenue from between the Maison Française and the
British Empire building stands as distinctively for New York as does
the now vernacular architecture of Rockefeller Center itself.

In Madison Square, at Fifth Avenue between 23rd and 26th Streets,
is the *Farragut Monument,* 1880–1881, by Augustus Saint-Gaudens
with a base by Stanford White. It is the first mature work by one of
the important New York sculptors of the last century: the low relief
carving on the base reflects the grace of Botticelli, of whom Saint-
Gaudens was fond, and the flowing lines of the sea are often cited as
foreshadowing continental Art Nouveau.

Park Avenue is famous for its tall glass-fronted office buildings, of
which Lever House built in 1950–1952 by the architectural firm of
Skidmore, Owings, and Merrill, is the first. The blue-green glass and
stainless steel façade helped establish the sleek-surfaced curtain-wall
architecture that today characterizes most of Manhattan Island. In the
space beneath the straight, narrow slab of the building is an area set
off by stainless steel supporting columns. Here there is usually an art
exhibit where contemporary painting and sculpture may be seen and
purchased.

The Union Carbide building between 47th and 48th Streets on Park
Avenue, also by Skidmore, Owings and Merrill, is another great monument of glass wall architecture featuring a black metal and stainless
steel covering as it rises 52 stories from a pink terrazzo plaza.

The most distinguished building on the avenue, however, is the
118 magnificent Seagram Building designed by Ludwig Mies van der
Rohe and Philip Johnson and completed in 1958. From the amber-

117. The United
Nations Building

grey glass and dark bronze exterior attached to a clearly expressed
skeleton frame, to the travertine walls and Italian glass mosaic ceiling
of the interior, the entire building was architect-designed right down
to the door knobs. It is the culminating example of the skyscraper
since its beginnings with Louis Sullivan. The very best in modern
technology and mass production methods are combined with the
choicest of materials assembled with great care and sensitivity to design and proportion, resulting in a true masterpiece of modern architecture. In its emphasis on formal beauty rather than on strict function
the Seagram has set a trend in large urban architecture.

The United Nations headquarters is at the East River between 42nd 117
and 48th Streets. The huge Secretariat building was to set a trend for
so-called 'glass box' architecture throughout the world. It was designed by Wallace K. Harrison and Max Abramovitz (U.S.A.) with an
international Board of Design Consultants including Le Corbusier
(France), Oscar Niemeyer (Brazil), Nikolai Bassov (U.S.S.R.) and
Sven Markelius (Sweden). A tour is available which allows one to see
the large stained glass memorial to Dag Hammarskjöld by Marc
Chagall and the Fernand Léger murals on the walls of the General

Assembly's meeting hall.

Certainly the best known church in New York City is St. Patrick's Cathedral on Fifth Avenue between 50th and 51st Streets – the first major cathedral in America built in the Gothic revival style. It was begun in 1853 by James Renwick (1818–1895) after designs based on Cologne Cathedral, with an interior reminiscent of Amiens, and an elaborate system of vaults which follows such English prototypes as York, Exeter and Westminster Abbey. The stained glass was made in Chartres and Nantes, then shipped to New York.

The largest and finest of New York's parks is Central Park, a rectangular area of lakes, ponds and streams, winding paths, and green pasture set in the very centre of Manhattan Island. A large quantity of statuary will be found ornamenting the various entrances to the park and scattered throughout its 840 acres – though there will be room here to mention only a few of the more prominent. Designed in 1858 by Frederick Law Olmsted and Calvert Vaux, the entire park is man-made. Every hill, valley, and plateau is part of a carefully worked out design called the 'Greensward' plan which won a competition set by the City in the spring of 1857. In sharp contrast to the formal gardens popular in the 18th century, Central Park exemplifies the 19th century English Romantic tradition of picturesque landscape, 'natural' and 'wild'. Though a number of 'improvements' have been made since the park's completion – not all of them in keeping with the original idea of an unspoiled natural environment – Central Park remains basically divided into two sections. The lower half is flat and pastoral, while the northern half is more picturesque with rock formations and dense woods.

Much of Central Park's sculpture is to be found in the southern half, beginning with the Pulitzer *Fountain of Abundance* designed by the architects Carrère and Hastings and with a huge bronze female personification of Abundance by Karl Bitter in the centre. Saint-Gaudens' *General Sherman* monument at the Plaza entrance to the Park at 59th Street is one of the most famous and conspicuous sculptures in the country. A block to the west, at Sixth Avenue and Central Park South, are three large bronze equestrian figures representing *Simon Bolivar, José Marti* and *José de San Martin,* the great liberators of the South American republics, which are gifts from their respective governments. Further west at Columbus Circle between Central Park South and Central Park West is the *Maine Memorial* designed by H. van Buren

118. (opposite) The Seagram Building

K. (opposite) Charles Demuth,
 I Saw the Figure 5 in Gold, 1928
 oil on composition board
 36 × 29¾ in. (91·4 × 75·5 cm.)
 The Metropolitan Museum of Art

119. The Bethesda Fountain
by Emma Stebbins

Magonigle in 1901–1913 with sculptures by Attilio Piccirilli which must rate among the finest of their kind in the city. Along the tree-lined promenade that leads to the Central Park Mall there are statues of *Columbus, Shakespeare, Robert Burns* and *Sir Walter Scott.* The Shakespeare by J. A. Q. Ward is an outstanding piece, and the same sculptor's *Indian Fighter,* at the south end of the promenade, is cited as one of the finest in the park. The northern end of the Mall terminates in a brick plaza graced by Emma Stebbins' *Bethesda Fountain,* the only 119 piece of statuary that figures in the original plan of Olmsted and Vaux. At the north end of the Conservatory Pond is an over life-size statue of *Hans Christian Anderson,* 1956, by Georg Lober, and not far away is the popular *Alice in Wonderland* by José de Creeft, its bronze surfaces kept shiny from the hundreds of children who daily crawl lovingly over Alice and her friends. The exotic obelisk behind the Metropolitan Museum of Art was made under the reign of Thotmes III about 1600 B.C. In 1880 it was shipped to Staten Island; from there it was floated on pontoons to East 96th Street and rolled to its present site on cannon balls. It is popularly known as Cleopatra's needle. A work of high quality is the self-portrait statue of *Albert Thorvaldsen* (1768–1844) which shows the Danish sculptor holding a hammer and chisel. It was placed at the 96th Street and Fifth Avenue entrance by American Danes. Other sculptures, monuments and memorials too numerous to mention are dotted throughout the park. Some of them are boring clichés, others downright bad, and still others are a pleasure to

120. The Lincoln Centre

stumble upon and a joy to return to.

120   Lincoln Center for the Performing Arts, opened in September o
1962, is New York's newest cultural centre. The fountain in the main
plaza with its 568 jets and 88 underwater lights was designed b
Philip Johnson and operatres automatically from programmed tape
Inside Philharmonic Hall, designed by Max Abramovitz, is Richard
Lippold's *Orpheus and Apollo,* a 5-ton 'space sculpture' made from
strips of highly polished copper alloy hung like huge ribbons from
their stainless steel wires and extending the entire length of the 190
foot Grand Promenade. On the plaza level stands Seymour Lipton's
Archangel, a 9-foot high abstraction made of bronze and Monel metal
On the same level Dmitri Hadzi's 10-foot cast bronze *K. 458 The Hun*
derives its title from Mozart's quartet of the same name. A large Henry
Moore shape in bronze reclines in the centre of a shallow pool between Philharmonic Hall and the Vivian Beaumont Theatre. In front
of the Library and Museum of the Performing Arts is Calder's *Le*
Guichet (The Ticket Window), a large black stabile supported by five
finger-like projections. Through the tall semi-circular arches of the
façade of Wallace K. Harrison's Metropolitan Opera House one can
see two huge murals by Marc Chagall, one a bright red, the other
yellow, with his characteristic dream-like floating figures. The
Museum of the Performing Arts is open weekdays 10 a.m. to 9 p.m.
Saturdays 10 a.m. to 6 p.m. and holidays 1 p.m. to 6 p.m.

Further north, on Central Park West at 77th Street, is the American

Museum of Natural History with its colossal Roman triumphal style façade by John Russell Pope who also designed the delicate colonnade court in the Frick mansion. The older part of the building facing 77th Street is a good example of Romanesque revival in the style of Henry Hobson Richardson. The museum itself is one of the oldest and most famous in the City. It possesses one of the earliest and best collections of American Indian art in the world, with a large display of northwest coast wood carvings, Iroquois face masks, and Plains Indian clothing and decoration. In the entrance hall on the main floor are three fine sculptured groups in bronze by Carl Akeley collectively entitled *The Lion Hunt*. At the entrance to the African exhibit are two African native dancers, a male and a female, by Malvina Hoffman, which are among the finest and most accurate realist sculptures in the city. The huge equestrian statue of *Theodore Roosevelt*, 1939, in front of the entrance is by J. E. Fraser.

Upper Fifth Avenue is famous for its large town houses built as private residences in the beginning of this century by wealthy New Yorkers in styles ranging from French Gothic to Italian Renaissance. One of the best remaining examples of an old town house in Gothic style is the Augustus Stuyvesant House (now the Ukranian Institute of America) on the south corner of 79th Street at Fifth Avenue. With its pointed gables, carved gargoyles and elaborate traceried designs in stone, it contrasts markedly with the James B. Duke mansion on the northeast corner of 78th Street and Fifth Avenue, built 1910–1912 by Horace Trombauer in the French Classic style of Louis XV. Notable for its magnificent marble staircase, gilded woodwork, and oak-panelled library, the building now houses the New York University Institute of Fine Arts. The department of conservation located in the basement prepares interesting exhibits relating to preservation and conservation of art works. Permission to visit the Duke mansion may be obtained at the receptionist desk in the lobby.

The long thin strip of park that separates Riverside Drive from the Hudson River on Manhattan's upper west side, also the work of Olmsted and Vaux, is one of the most pleasant parts of the island, affording frequent views of the river and of the grand old apartment houses along the Drive. There are numerous statues in the park, celebrating personalities from Joan of Arc to Louis Kossuth, Hungarian patriot. One of the two most prominent monuments is the *Sailors and Soldiers Memorial* at 89th Street and the Drive, which consists of an enormous circular array of Corinthian columns centred on a white marble terrace inlaid with red sandstone. White marble steps and balustrades lead from the Park to the Drive. The monument was built in 1900 by the City of New York to commemorate the valour of the Union army of the Civil War. *Grant's Tomb* is a formal Roman-style mausoleum where the 18th president and his wife are buried in two enormous diorite sarcophagi. On the way to Grant's Tomb at 122nd Street and the Drive one can conveniently stop at Anna Hyatt Huntington's equestrian figure of *Joan of Arc* erected on a base containing fragments from Reims Cathedral and stones from the tower of Rouen where the Maid awaited trial and death (93rd Street and Riverside Drive). A little further north at 100th Street is the *Fireman's Memorial* with its large low-relief of a horse-drawn fire wagon by Attilio Piccirilli.

Opposite Grant's Tomb is Riverside Church completed in 1929 and resembling Chartres Cathedral in general design. The stained glass windows are among the finest in the City; those in the clerestory of the nave are duplicates of the clerestory windows at Chartres. A large *Madonna and Child* and a *Christ in Majesty* on the south wall of the nave are by Sir Jacob Epstein. The delicately carved white chancel screen and the intricate reredos in Christ Chapel are excellent works in stone.

The other great Gothic church on the upper West Side is the Cathedral of St John the Divine, which like Antonio Gaudi's Cathedral of the Sagrada Familia in Barcelona, unfortunately has become an anachronism and will never be finished. Located at Cathedral Parkway from 110th to 113th Streets, the impressive size of the building, with its large buttresses, dominates several blocks. Especially notable is the fine vaulting of St Martin's Chapel where there is another statue of *Joan of Arc* executed in marble by Anna Hyatt Huntington.

121   The Low Memorial Library of Columbia University at West 116th Street between Broadway and Amsterdam Avenue, modelled after the Pantheon in Rome and built by McKim, Mead and White in 1893–1897, was once considered one of the most beautiful buildings in America. On the front steps sits Daniel Chester French's colossal bronze *Alma Mater,* 1902–1903, dressed in classical garb with an idealized facial expression. In the lobby of Columbia's Uris Hall is an excellent metal assemblage sculpture by Clark B. Fitz-Gerald called *Business and Society,* 1965. Both 'found' and 'created' objects are combined with great sensitivity to texture and design on a huge wrought-iron screen and arranged in bands of compartmentalized scenes radiating from the centre and telling the story of man's progress in a business society.

121. The Low Memorial Library

The Jumel Mansion in Roger Morris Park at West 160th Street and Edgecomb Avenue is one of the most interesting Georgian colonial houses in the City. The two-story portico and railing atop the hipped roof make it an outstanding and rare example of its type. Now a museum, there are paintings, furnishings and historic relics on display inside.

The only existing 18th century farmhouse in New York City is the two-story typically Dutch Colonial Dyckman House at 204th Street and Broadway. Built in 1748 and rebuilt after a fire in 1783, it is now a museum with period furnishings and exhibits relating to colonial New York.

This much too brief description barely scratches the surface of Manhattan's art, much of which lies ensconced in little-known churches, out-of-the-way museums, historic houses, in college buildings, in tiny parks crowded in by threatening skyscrapers and in private collections. And all this is without even mentioning the four other boroughs—Brooklyn, Queens, Bronx and Staten Island, which have their own museums, more and better colonial architecture and excellent parks with numerous monuments.

Art for Sale

For those who are not content merely to look at objects under the watchful eye of the museum guards, there are well over 400 commercial art galleries in New York City where viewers can become owners of anything from Old Masters to psychedelic assemblages

The majority of these galleries are owned and operated by individuals, many of whom are recognized specialists in a particular field of art. Most galleries maintain public exhibition rooms and hang changing shows that are open to the public.

The City's two major art auction houses, Parke-Bernet and Plaza Galleries, are both located uptown. Their annual business runs well into the millions as they supply art museums and galleries throughout the world. The three largest and most varied in their holdings, with works ranging from Medieval to the 20th century, are Knoedler, Wildenstein (both established in the 19th century) and Marlborough-Gerson — probably the richest of the three. They all hold important exhibitions and publish equally important catalogues.

Most of Manhattan's galleries are located in one of three distinct areas: between 65th and 85th Streets on Madison Avenue, on 57th Street east and slightly west of Fifth Avenue, and on 10th Street around Third Avenue in Greenwich Village.

57th Street is the original gallery section of the City. As rents and taxes rose and competition became more fierce many moved uptown on Madison Avenue, and more recently, in the wake of the museum cluster about the Metropolitan, many have gathered around 79th Street and Madison. Some, like Knoedler, Marlborough-Gerson, Pierre Matisse, Loeb and others, have stayed put. Most of the 57th Street galleries and those in the general area like Janis, Downtown, and Betty Parsons deal in expensive modern classics and are no place for bargain hunting or weekend specials.

Madison Avenue galleries can be quite as 'established' and just as expensive, though sometimes with more pretence and less justification for it. There is usually the suave young man impeccably dressed and trained to say just so much and no more, to be polite and efficient but never too informative. Owners are often very busy and tend to be quick and to the point, especially in the better galleries. There are literally hundreds of galleries of all descriptions on Madison Avenue, nearly all of them welcome browsers, and prospective buyers even more. The quality varies greatly from old establishments like Durlacher Brothers, Perls, Saidenberg and Parke-Bernet to cheap frame shops and dealers in over-priced junk jewellery.

In Greenwich Village taxes are lower, profits are generally less, there are fewer neckties and more animation. Here gallery people often tend to have more than their share of opinions so that conversation needn't lag. Many Village galleries are 'co-ops', the result of several artists' joint effort to get their work in the public eye, hence these owners too are experts in their field.

A history of innovation reaches all the way back to Alfred Stieglitz' '291' Gallery and to Gertrude Whitney's 'Studio Club'; both were landmarks in American art and both were located in the Village. The present hub of activity is on East 10th Street close to Third Avenue, where galleries hatch and die as artists 'make it' and move uptown or as bank accounts diminish. New movements are often born here, launched in co-ops and later taken up by the older galleries.

Galleries, museums and sale rooms

The following list gives addresses and telephone numbers of about 100 commercial galleries in Manhattan with a brief description of the kind of art each deals in. The Yellow Pages of the Manhatten Telephone Directory list many more. Shows, openings and other information may be found in the New Yorker Magazine, Cue Magazine and the Sunday New York Times. The Art Gallery Magazine published, monthly from October to June, describes shows in galleries across the country as well as in New York City. The ultimate pedigree for an art gallery is membership in the Art Dealers Association of America, which occurs only through invitation. A list of members can be obtained at no charge. The art season in New York traditionally runs from October to June. Most galleries are closed during July and August. **The hours are usually from 10 a.m. to 5 p.m. Tuesday through Saturday.**

1 **A.C.A. Gallery**
63 E. 57 St   PL 5–9622
Modern paintings, sculpture and graphics, especially American Realist and Social Protest

2 **Acquavella Galleries**
119 E. 57 St   PL 3–1296
European and American Old and Modern paintings

3 **American Indian Arts Centre**
1051 3rd Ave.   UN 1–2630
Representative works of leading American Indian and Eskimo artists and sculptors. Navajo rugs, Hopi Kachina dolls, Zuni, Hopi and Navajo silverwork

4 **Associated American Artists**
605 5th Ave.   PL 5–4211
International old master and modern etchings, lithographs, woodcuts

5 **Art Fair**
123 2nd Ave.   OR 4–6545
Contemporary American paintings, graphics and sculpture

6 **Babcock**
805 Madison Ave.   LE 5–9355
Modern paintings and graphics, Americana.

7 **Bianchini**
50 W. 57 St   582–0153
Modern paintings, graphics and sculpture

8 **Bodley**
787 Madison Ave.   AG 9–2155

*Modern paintings, graphics and
sculpture, especially Surrealism
and Modern Master
drawings*

9 Bonino
7 W. 57 St   PL 2–9556–7–8
*Contemporary European, American
and South American paintings
and sculpture*

10 Borgenicht
1018 Madison Ave   LE 5–8040
*Modern American paintings,
drawings and sculpture*

11 Byron
1018 Madison Ave   YU 8–9570
*Contemporary American and
European graphics and sculpture;
pre-Columbian art*

12 Julius Carlebach
1040 Madison Ave   RE 7–0116
*Oriental, Ancient and Primitive art
(pre-Columbian and African),
antique jewellery and chess sets*

13 Leo Castelli
4 E. 77 St   BU 8–4820
*Modern paintings, graphics and
sculpture, especially up to the
minute movements*

14 Chapellier
943 Madison Ave
also 22 E. 80 St   988–8430
*Early American and early 20th
century American painting,
especially the Eight*

15 Cordier and Ekstrom
978 Madison Ave   YU 8–8857
Modern paintings and sculpture

16 D'arcy
1091 Madison Ave   BU 8–5750
*Modern paintings and sculpture,
Primitive art*

17 Davis
231 E. 60 St   PL 3–5420
*Contemporary American and turn
of the century American art; 19th
century English watercolours*

18 Peter Deitsch
24 E. 81 St   RE 7–8279
*19th and 20th century original
European and American prints and
drawings*

19 Terry Dintenfass
18 E. 67 St   RH 4–1580
*Contemporary American
(figurative) paintings, graphics
and sculpture*

20 Downtown
465 Park Ave (Ritz Concourse)
PL 3–3707
*20th century American masters in
painting, sculpture and graphics,
also American folk art*

21 Durlacher Bros.
538 Madison Ave   EL 5–3398
*Old Master drawings and
contemporary American paintings*

22 Dwan
29 W. 57th St   753–9280
*Modern paintings, and sculpture,
especially contemporary*

23 East Hampton
22 W. 56 St   CI 6–3218
*Contemporary American and
Canadian paintings, graphics and
sculpture, especially Op and
Visionary*

24 Charles Egan
41 E. 57 St   PL 5–1825
*20th century paintings and
especially contemporary sculpture*

25 Robert Elkon
1063 Madison Ave   LE 5–3940
*20th century European and
American masters in painting and
sculpture, especially strong in
work of new artists*

26 André Emmerich
41 E. 57 St   PL 2–0124
*Contemporary international
paintings and sculpture;
pre-Columbian and Classical art*

27 Far
746 Madison Ave   RE 4–7287

Contemporary American and
European paintings, graphics and
sculpture, especially 19th and
20th century drawings

28 Richard Feigen
24 E. 81 St   RE 7–6640
European and American
contemporaries

29 Herbert E. Feist
1125 Madison Ave   UN 1–8362
Old and Modern Master drawings
and frames

30 Findlay
11–13 E. 57 St   PL 8–1297
Modern European paintings and
graphics

31 Fischbach Gallery
29 W. 57 St   PL 9–2345
Modern American paintings,
graphics and sculpture, especially
newest styles

32 Forum
1018 Madison Ave   LE 5–6080
Contemporary American figurative
paintings, sculpture and drawings

33 French & Co.
978 Madison Ave   LE 5–3330
European fine and decorative arts
from the Renaissance to the
present day, especially tapestries
and 18th century furniture

34 Allan Frumkin
41 E. 57 St   PL 3–3180
20th century European and
American paintings and sculpture.
Heavy in modern drawings,
especially German Expressionist

35 Galerie St Etienne
24 W. 57 St   CI 5–6734
American and European paintings,
graphics and sculpture, especially
Austrian and German
Expressionists and 19th and 20th
century American primitives

36 Galleria Odyssia
41 E. 57 St   HA 1–3690

Modern paintings and sculpture;
some graphics

37 Lucien Goldschmidt
1117 Madison Ave   TR 9–0070
Drawings, prints and lithographs,
illustrated books, manuscripts

38 Grand Central Moderns
8 W. 56 St   TN 7–3344
Modern American paintings from
Abstract Expressionism on. Also
sculpture and other media

39 Graham
1014 Madison Ave   LE 5–5767
Paintings by 20th century
American masters

40 Greer
35 W. 53 St   CI 6–1555
Modern European and American
paintings, sculpture and graphics

41 Stephen Hahn Gallery
960 Madison Ave   LE 5–3520
19th and 20th century French
master paintings

42 Hirschl & Adler
21 E. 67 St   LE 5–8810
19th and 20th century European
and American figurative paintings
and sculpture

43 Leonard Hutton
787 Madison Ave   AG 9–9700
German Expressionist paintings
and sculpture, French Cubist
paintings

44 Iolas
15 E. 55 St   PL 5–6778
Surrealist and modern paintings
and sculpture

45 Martha Jackson Gallery
32 E. 69 St   YU 8–1800
Contemporary International
painting, sculpture and graphics

46 Sidney Janis Gallery
15 E. 57 St   PL 9–4241
Modern European and American
master paintings, graphics and
sculpture

47 Kennedy
20 E. 56 St   355–3740
*Modern American paintings,
graphics and sculpture, especially
Americana. Strong in American
and European graphics and early
American figurative painting*

48 J. J. Klejman
982 Madison Ave   LE 5–5484
Primitive and archaeological art

49 Knoedler
14 E. 57 St   PL 3–9742
*Old Masters, contemporary
painting and sculpture*

50 Komor
19 E. 71 St   TR 9–3840
*Oriental, primitive (African, pre-
Columbian) and some medieval.
Best to call for an appointment*

51 Kornblee
58 E. 79 St   UN 1–4245
*Modern American painting and
sculpture*

52 Kraushaar
1055 Madison Ave (entrance on
80th St)   LE 5–9888
*Largely early 20th century and
contemporary American paintings
and sculpture*

53 La Boetie
1042 Madison Ave   535–4865
*20th century European and
American paintings, naïve art and
sculpture*

54 Landau-Alan
766 Madison Ave   535–3113
*Contemporary Europeans and
Americans in all media, especially
younger artists*

55 Lefebre
47 E. 77 St   RH 4–3384
*Modern European paintings,
graphics and sculpture, with
emphasis on latest developments*

56 Albert Loeb and Krugier
12 E. 57 St   PL 3–7857

*19th century European paintings
and sculpture; modern European
and American paintings, sculpture
and graphics*

57 Royal Marks Gallery
19 E. 71 St   UN 1–3400
*20th century European and
American masters in painting,
graphics and sculpture*

58 Marlborough-Gerson Gallery
41 E. 57 St   PL 2–5353
*Chiefly 19th and 20th century
European and American
paintings*

59 Mi Chou
801 Madison Ave   YU 8–1840
*Oriental painting and calligraphy
from the 15th through the 20th
centuries*

60 Milch
21 E. 67 St   BU 8–2770
*19th and 20th century American
paintings and watercolours,
mostly representational*

61 Pierre Matisse Gallery
41 E. 57 St   EL 5–6269
*20th century masters in European
and American paintings and
sculpture*

62 Midtown
11 E. 57 St   PL 8–1900
*Contemporary American painting,
graphics and sculpture, largely
representational*

63 Multiples
929 Madison Ave   249–3250
*Objects, banners, graphics by
established contemporary artists in
signed and limited editions*

64 Oestreicher's Prints
43 W. 46 St   PL 7–1190–1
*Large selection of graphics and
reproductions from all over the
world*

65 Tibor de Nagy
29 W. 57 St   421–3780

Contemporary sculptures and paintings, both abstract and representational

66 Niveau
962 Madison Ave   RE 7–1094
20th century American and European paintings

67 Nordness
134 E. 70 St   TR 9–2250
Contemporary international paintings, graphics and sculpture

68 Pace
9 W. 57 St   HA 1–3292
Contemporary European and American painting and especially sculpture

69 Parke-Bernet
980 Madison Ave   TR 9–8300
All types of art from all periods sold at frequent auctions

70 Betty Parsons
24 W. 57 St   CI 7–7480
Modern paintings, graphics and sculpture, chiefly American abstract and hard-edge paintings

71 Perls
1016 Madison Ave   TR 9–7440
20th century American and European master paintings and sculpture, no young unknowns

72 Phoenix
939 Madison Ave   RH 4–5166
Contemporary paintings and sculpture, including psychedelic work

73 Plaza
406 E. 79 St   TR 9–1800
Large art auction house – all periods, mediums, styles

74 Poindexter
21 W. 56 St   JU 6–6630
American contemporary painting and sculpture

75 Poster Centre
16 E. 78 St   861–0422

Classical European and American posters

76 Frank Rehn
655 Madison Ave   PL 3–4694
Modern and contemporary American paintings, graphics and sculpture, especially early 20th century

77 Roko
645 Madison Ave   PL 2–0390
Modern American paintings, graphics and sculpture of all styles; Japanese prints and scrolls

78 Rosenberg
20 E. 79 St   RH 4–2340
19th and 20th century European and American painting and sculpture, especially French 19th century paintings, mostly representational

79 Saidenberg
1035 Madison Ave   BU 8–3387
20th century American and European paintings, sculpture and graphics.

80 Harry Salpeter
42 E. 57 St   MU 8–5659
American paintings, graphics and sculpture, mostly representational

81 William H. Schab
48 E. 57 St   PL 8–0327
Extensive collection of prints, especially Old Masters

82 Bertha Schaefer
41 E. 57 St   755–3330
20th century abstract American and European paintings, graphics and sculpture

83 Walter Schatzki
153 E. 57 St   MU 8–6116
Old prints, maps, watercolours and drawings

84 Schoelkopf
825 Madison Ave   TR 9–4638
Contemporary European and American paintings, graphics and

sculpture

85 Sculpture Centre
167 E. 69 St   RE 7–9870
*Contemporary American sculpture
exclusively*

86 Segy
708 Lexington Ave   EL 5–3859
*Authentic antique African
sculpture*

87 Jacques Seligmann and Co.
5 E. 57 St   PL 3–0250
*Old Masters. Contemporary
painting by appointment only*

88 E & A Silberman
1014 Madison Ave   TR 9–6980
*Old and Modern Masters,
European and American*

89 Charles E. Slatkin
115 E. 92 St   LE 4–4222
*Old Master and early 20th century
drawings, sculpture by Rodin
and Bourdelle*

90 Stable
33 E. 74th St   RE 7–0100
*Contemporary paintings and
sculpture*

91 Staempfli
47 E. 77 St   LE 5–1919
*Modern American and European
painting and sculpture,
representational and abstract*

92 Allan Stone
48 E. 86 St   YU 8–6870
*Contemporary American paintings
and sculpture. Newest movements*

93 E. V. Thaw & Co.
525 Park Ave   LE 5–6333
*Master drawings and paintings of
all periods; by appointment only*

94 Catherine Viviano
42 E. 57 St   PL 8–1030
*Contemporary European and
American paintings, graphics and
sculpture*

95 Waddell
15 E. 57 St   421–4141
*European and American
contemporary painting and sculptures,
especially most recent styles*

96 Weintraub
1193 Lexington Ave   TR 9–1195
*Modern European painting,
watercolours, graphics and
sculpture*

97 Wildenstein
19 E. 64 St   TR 9–0500
*Venerable Masters of European
and American painting*

98 Willard
29 E. 72 St   RH 4–2925
*Modern American and European
paintings and sculpture*

99 Howard Wise
50 W. 57 St   CO 5–0465
*Contemporary art, with emphasis
on Kinetic and Light art*

100 Zabriskie
699 Madison Ave   832–9034
*Modern American paintings and
sculpture; figurative and abstract*

101 Zegri
10 E. 8 St   GR 3–7510
*Contemporary Latin American
painting, sculpture and graphics*

Museums

102 Metropolitan Museum of Art
Fifth Avenue at 82nd Street
Telephone: TRafalgar 9–5500
Open hours: Monday, Wednesday,
Thursday, Friday 10–5; Tuesday
10–10; Sundays and holidays 1–5

103 Cloisters
Fort Tryon Park
Telephone: WAdsworth 3–3700
Open hours: 10–5 Tuesdays thru
Saturdays; 1–5 Sundays and
holidays; closed Mondays

104 The Frick Collection
One East 70th Street
Telephone: BUtterfield 8–0700
Open hours: 10–6 Tuesdays thru
Saturdays; 1–6
Sundays and holidays; closed
Mondays; also January 1st, May
30th, July 4th, Thanksgiving Day,
December 24th and 25th. In June,
July and August: open 1–6
Wednesdays and Saturdays;
Thursdays, Fridays, and Saturdays
10–6; closed Mondays and
Tuesdays

105 The Audubon Terrace
Broadway between 155th and
156th Streets
Including:
American Geographical Society
Telephone: ADirondack 4–8100
Open hours: 9–4.45 Mondays
thru Fridays
American Numismatic Society
Telephone: AUdubon 6–3030
Open hours: 10–5 Tuesdays thru
Saturdays
Closed Sundays, Mondays and
holidays
Museum of the American Indian
Telephone: AUdubon 3–2420
Open hours: 1–5 Tuesdays thru
Sundays
Closed Mondays and holidays
The Hispanic Society of America
Telephone: WAdsworth 6–2234

Open hours: 10–4.30 Tuesdays
thru Saturdays
2–5 Sundays
Closed Mondays and major holidays

106 The Museum of Modern Art
11 West 53rd Street
Telephone: CIrcle 5–8900
Open hours: 11–6 daily
12 noon to 6 Sundays
11–9 Thursdays
Closed Christmas Day

107 The Jewish Museum
1109 Fifth Avenue at 92nd Street
Telephone: RIverside 9–3770
Open hours: 12 noon to 5
Mondays thru Thursdays
11–3 Fridays
11–6 Sundays
Closed Saturdays

108 The Solomon R. Guggenheim Museum
1071 Fifth Avenue at 89 Street
Telephone: ENright 9–5110
Open hours: 10–6 Tuesdays thru
Saturdays
10–9 Thursdays
12 noon–6 Sundays and all
holidays
Closed Mondays (except
holidays), July 4th and Christmas

109 Gallery of Modern Art including the Huntington Hartford Collection
Two Columbus Circle
Telephone: LT 1–2311
Open hours: 11–7 Tuesdays thru
Saturdays
12 noon–6 Sundays and holidays
Closed Mondays

110 Whitney Museum of American Art
945 Madison Avenue at 75th Street
Telephone: 249–4100
Open hours: 11–5 daily
12 noon–5 Sundays
Closed Christmas Day

111 The Pierpont Morgan Library
29–33 East 36th Street at
Madison Avenue

Telephone: MUrray Hill 5–0008
Open hours: 9.30–5 Mondays
thru Saturdays
Closed Sundays and holidays;
also Saturdays during July, as
well as the entire month of August

112 The New York Public Library
Fifth Avenue and 42nd Street
Telephone: OXford 5–4200
Open hours: 9–10 Mondays thru
Saturdays
1–10 Sundays and holidays

113 The New York Historical Society
170 Central Park West at 77th
Street
Telephone: TRafalgar 3–3400
Open hours: 1–5 weekdays and
Sundays
10–5 Saturdays
Closed Mondays, holidays and the
entire month of August

114 Museum of the City of New York
Fifth Avenue between 103rd and
104th Streets
Telephone: LEhigh 4–1672
Open hours: 10–5 Tuesday thru
Saturdays
1–5 Sundays and holidays
Closed Mondays

115 New York City Hall
City Hall Park
Open hours: 10–4 Mondays thru
Fridays
Closed Saturdays, Sundays and
holidays

116 Riverside Museum
310 Riverside Drive at 103rd
Street
Telephone: UNiversity 4–1700
Open hours: 1–5 Tuesdays thru
Sundays
Closed Mondays, holidays and
during the months of July and
August

117 Nicholas Roerich Museum
319 West 107th Street
Telephone: UNiversity 4–7752

Open hours: 2–5 Sundays thru
Fridays
Closed Saturdays, holidays and
during the months of July and
August

118 Asia House Gallery
112 East 64th Street between
Park and Lexington Avenues
Telephone: PLaza 1–4210
Open hours: 10–5 Mondays thru
Fridays
11–5 Saturdays
11–5 Sundays and holidays

119 The Museum of Primitive Art
15 West 54th Street
Telephone: CIrcle 6–9493
Open hours: 12 noon–5 Tuesdays
thru Saturdays
1–5 Sundays
Closed Mondays

120 Museum of Early American Folk Arts
49 West 53rd Street
Telephone: LT 1–2474
Open hours: 10.30–5.30 Tuesdays
thru Sundays
Closed Mondays

121 Museum of Contemporary Crafts
29 West 53rd Street
Telephone: CIrcle 6–6840
Open hours: 12 noon–6 Mondays
thru Saturdays
2–6 Sundays

122 Cooper Union Museum for the Decorative Arts
Cooper Square and Seventh Street
Telephone: ALgonquin 4–6300
Open hours: 10–5 weekends
Closed on major holidays,
February 12th, December 24th
and 31st and on Saturdays from
June 1st to October 1st

123 The Brooklyn Museum
Eastern Parkway and Washington
Avenue, Brooklyn
Telephone: NEvins 8–5000
Open hours: 10–5 Mondays thru
Saturdays
1–5 Sundays and holidays

Credits

During the writing of this book it was necessary to refer to and to seek the aid of numerous other books, articles and pamphlets. The following books are those upon which I depended most heavily for factual and historical information.

Janson, H. W., *History of Art*, Abrams, New York, 1962.

Murray, Peter and Linda, *A Dictionary of Art and Artists*, Penguin Books, London, 1963.

Haftmann, Werner, *Painting in the Twentieth Century*, Praeger, New York, 1960.

Green, Samuel, *American Art – A Historical Survey*, Ronald, New York, 1966.

Flexner, James Thomas, *A Short History of American Painting*, Houghton Mifflin Company, New York, 1950.

Chanin, A. L., *Art Guide/New York*, Horizon Press, New York, 1965.

Howe, Winifred E., *A History of the Metropolitan Museum of Art*, New York, 1913.

Wehle, Harry B., The Metropolitan Museum of Art, *A Catalogue of Italian, Spanish and Byzantine Paintings*, New York, 1940.

Wehle, Harry B., and Salinger, Margaretta M., The Metropolitan Museum of Art, *A Catalogue of Early Flemish, Dutch and German Paintings*, New York, 1947.

Sterling, Charles, *The Metropolitan Museum of Art, A Catalogue of French Paintings XV-XVIII Centuries*, Harvard University Press, Cambridge (Mass.), 1955.

Art, *A Catalogue of French Paintings XV-XVIII Centuries*, Harvard University Press, Cambridge (Mass.), 1955.

Sterling, Charles, and Salinger, Margaretta M., *French Paintings, A Catalogue of the Collection of the Metropolitan Museum of Art, III, XIX-XX Centuries*, New York, 1967.

Gardner, Albert Ten Eyck, and Feld, Stuart P., *American Paintings, A Catalogue of the Collection of the Metropolitan Museum of Art, I, Painters born by 1815*, New York, 1965.

Geldzahler, Henry, *American Painting in the Twentieth Century*, The Metropolitan Museum of Art, New York, 1965.

Rorimer, James J., *The Cloisters*, The Metropolitan Museum of Art, New York, 1963.

The Frick Collection, An Illustrated Catalogue of the Works of Art in the Collection of Henry Clay Frick, Pittsburgh, 1949.

Handbook of the Hispanic Society of America, New York, 1938.

Barr, Alfred H., *Masters of Modern Art*, The Museum of Modern Art, New York, 1954.

A Handbook to the Solomon R. Guggenheim Museum Collection, New York, 1959.

Goodrich, Lloyd, and Baur, John I. H., *American Art of our Century*, published for the Whitney Museum of American Art by Frederick A. Praeger, New York, 1961.

Burnham, Alan (ed.), *New York Landmarks*, published under the auspices of the Municipal Art Society of New York, Wesleyan University Press, Middletown, Connecticut, 1961.

United States Works Progress Administration, *New York City Guide* (American Guide Series), Random House, New York, 1939.

Grateful acknowledgement is made to the Museum of Modern Art for permission to use the quote appearing on p. 100 from *Masters of Modern Art* by Alfred H. Barr, Jr.

Acknowledgement also is made to the various articles in the *Bulletin* of the Metropolitan Museum of Art, the 'Guide to the Collections' series of booklets of the Metropolitan, and to the various periodicals published by the Brooklyn Museum.

See pages 184–191 for addresses and further information

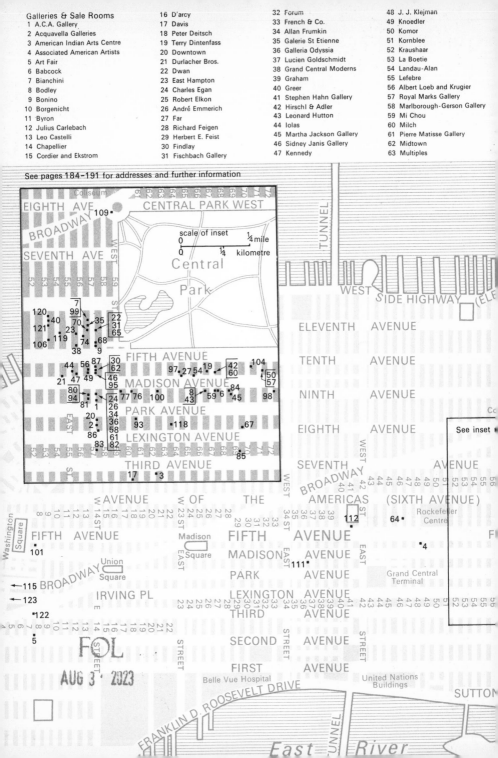